When People Grieve

Other Books by Paula D'Arcy

Sacred Threshold / Crossing the Inner Barrier to a Deeper Love (The Crossroad Publishing Company, 2004)

Seeking With All My Heart / Encountering God's Presence Today (The Crossroad Publishing Company, 2003)

A New Set of Eyes / Discovering the Hidden God (The Crossroad Publishing Company, 2002)

Red Fire / A Quest for Awakening (Inner Ocean Press, 2001)

Gift of the Red Bird / The Story of a Divine Encounter (The Crossroad Publishing Company, 1996)

Where the Wind Begins / Stories of Hurting People Who Said Yes to Life (Harold Shaw / Random House, 1984)

Song for Sarah / A Mother's Journey Through Grief and Beyond (Harold Shaw / WaterBrook Press, 1979, 2001)

When People Grieve

Guidance for Grievers and the Friends Who Care

A completely revised and updated edition of
When Your Friend Is Grieving

Paula D'Arcy

A Crossroad Book
The Crossroad Publishing Company
New York

This printing: 2014

The Crossroad Publishing Company
www.CrossroadPublishing.com

Copyright © 1990, 2005 by Paula D'Arcy

Printed in the United States of America

The text of this book is set in 11/14 Korinna.
The display type is Calligraphic 431.

Cataloging-in-Publication Data is available from
the Library of Congress

ISBN 10: 0-8245-2339-3
ISBN 13: 978-08245-2339-8

Contents

For my daughter Beth Starr,

and for the members of
the First Congregational Church,
Watertown, Connecticut,
who were my bridge of love in 1975.

*If we carry our storms
like actors pretending to be brave,
each swallowed tear will fill our hearts
like a bag of stones.*

—Alison Asher

Those first days, sorrow's pain
was tangible:
an amputation, a dismemberment,
the gap so great, no sobs,
children, friends
would fill its space:
a broken heart is body's pain indeed.
Days pass, and nights, flowing into weeks;
milk no longer spills
with my tears.
Hours once spent weeping
now weave into patterns,
our words of grief and love
now reach for friendship's clasp,
now look ahead. . . .

—Lois Lake Church

From *Quarto,* written for Emily, 8/8/84

Love Is Up To Us

THIS IS A BOOK about loss and hope. Designed to instruct and encourage friends who want to help and support those who grieve, it also serves as a compassionate road map for the bereaved themselves. Its intention is healing. There are no perfect answers, nor any guaranteed how-to's. Hopefully the bereaved will find in these pages not only comfort and understanding but also something they can offer to friends, saying, *Here's what I'm going through and ways you can help.* The experience of learning about grief through the eyes and hearts of those who have known its sting enables all of us to face life's inevitable seasons of pain more sensitively and with greater confidence.

Grief is the heart's response to any deep loss. For the purpose of simplification this book will use stories of bereavement. Yet grief is all-inclusive. There are many deaths in life, and we grieve all of them. We mourn the loss of employment, the deaths of our pets, infertility, divorce, and each death and disappointment experienced within our relationships. We mourn moving from treasured homes or well-known geographies. We mourn the losses caused by aging and disease — the loss of bodily and mental control — as well as the physical signs of aging. We mourn the death of our dreams. We mourn losses set in motion by natural disasters and acts of terror. We grieve all endings on the way to new beginnings. And each grief changes us.

Many of the things written on these pages were learned during my heart's own journey with grief. And because we credit with authorship the person who has actually put the words onto the page, only my name is listed as the author of this book. But my unnamed coauthors are the thousands of fellow grievers I've met over the past thirty years. They allowed me to enter their hearts and private pain, confirming my own learning and experience. They are joined by the friends who made, and continue to form, my community — the ones who believed in me and accepted me in sorrow, just as I was, and taught me about the force of unconditional love. This book is our collective gift back to the world.

Learning to love deeply and truly changes our experience of living. The acclaimed writer and speaker Jim Wallis, in reflecting on the poverty and pain suffered by millions on this earth, acknowledges, "Maybe we are the ones we've been waiting for." No one else will make it happen. Love is up to us.

Loss

LATE MARCH in New England, and the air is chilly. I pull a loose cardigan sweater tighter across my chest and take a deep breath, following my sisters and my daughter Beth into the Old Stone Church. We are there to place flower arrangements for my mother's funeral in front of the large white-framed windows lining both sides of the old meetinghouse.

As I enter the room from the rear, my eyes search the worship space for a communion table where a larger arrangement of flowers will be set. But the table is temporarily hidden behind a confusion of microphones, chairs, speakers, keyboards — all remnants of an earlier rehearsal with the church's contemporary musicians. I walk around the tangle of chairs and equipment in a daze, unable to stop thinking that when my mother left her home three days earlier on her way to a senior exercise class, she intended to return. She intended to see this church again. She intended to swallow the single white pill she left waiting on the cutting board at the end of her kitchen counter, next to the drain board...the diuretic she faithfully took after exercising.

I marvel, now, at the symbol that untaken pill has become; not only a sign of my mother's interrupted routine, it's a symbol of the larger reality that our physical life on earth is stunningly tenuous. The breaths we take can suddenly not be taken. For every human being, there is a day, time, and place after which we are no longer alive.

Such a short while ago my mother's pill represented the ongoingness of things, her daily life...the classes and appointments that merged together to create her weeks and months. But lying there now, the pill is a bold reminder that everything physical is temporary. We live side by side with both birth and death.

Those who lack courage flee
from their storms and brag
about their swift, strong wings.
Only the bravest of the brave
will soar straight *into* the storm.
— Alison Asher

In the church that afternoon I eventually shook my thoughts aside and slowly began to clean the area in front of the altar space. As my sisters and Beth placed flowerpots on each of the broad windowsills, I folded chairs and slid music stands into dark corners. Clearing the clutter and trying to make a plain room beautiful was helpful. Something to *do,* something to *change,* in face of the one reality we *couldn't* change: in face of the amazing sense that one minute you are breathing and the next second you are not. It was something to *do* against the enormous realization that one day every chance to know the full delight of love will be gone. Suddenly there are no further moments in which to finally summon courage for your life or to rise up against the fears that limit you. Our chances to unmask fear eventually run out. One day, you don't go home again.

We arranged flowers that afternoon with full hearts. Then, weary, we returned to my mother's home. It was then I noticed the wooden calendar on my mother's kitchen table, a gift from me a Christmas ago. I had purchased it so her arthritic fingers would have exercise as she moved the number cubes each morning, creating the correct date. Beyond that, her memory would be stimulated as she concentrated on the day of the week, the month.... The calendar now read Monday, March 22, its blocks lined up straight, the wooden bird atop the blocks heralding the day. Only the present day was March 25, not March 22. Since my mother's fingers had last moved those cubes, life had moved on, finding its way to the next morning, and the one after that. But my mother had stopped following along. She had expected to return when she left the house on the morning of March 22. She had expected to live through not only the twenty-second, but also the twenty-third and all the days of March. And April. And for many more Mays.

In the days that followed, I repeatedly felt as if a great tide had come to pull me into deeper waters and that my mother was no longer there to obscure that greater reality. It was a surprising feeling for an adult woman who had left home years before and lived thousands of miles away from her parents. Nevertheless, a force that seemed intent on sending me out to sea, alone, was unmistakably drawing me. Everything was shifting. I felt as if I had formerly been tethered to a mooring, and now the line holding me to the dock had been untied, propelling me to new seas. *I did not choose this voyage,* I kept thinking. Yet there I was, in high seas, whether or not I wanted to be, buffeted from the inside and filled with a sense that the next step was to let go, for a second time in my life, and allow grief to take me to new places.

Just let go. The words swam in front of me like a refrain. *Let go. Don't hold on.* I knew why. Because when navigating the waters of grief, you don't prevail by opposing them. You prevail by surrendering to grief's wisdom. You agree to stand undefended before things that are not permanent and let pain pull you toward everything that lasts.

My friend Richard Rohr, the well-known Franciscan priest, wrote to me, "Don't avoid this 'wonderful/terrible grieving' by living out this experience as just 'missing your mother.' It is much deeper than that." He knew.

Another friend and author, Joyce Rupp, called the moment "this great farewell."

A greater farewell, I thought, than I'd guessed. Farewell not only to a person, but also, *again,* to a way of seeing and thinking that tries to convince me that change can be outwitted. Farewell to yet another veil. (How many veils does life present?) Farewell to everything in me that resists knowing the full force of life. Farewell, one more time, to the seduction of believing that personality, geography, and heritage are who I really am. Grief was sweeping me into her arms once again in order to correct my sight.

During the hard months following the deaths of my young husband, Roy, and our twenty-two-month-old daughter, Sarah, in 1975 — they were killed by a drunk driver in an accident that I survived — I thought grief and I had wrestled our seminal match. Pregnant with a second child at that time and feeling wildly alone and like a crazy woman inside, I'd walked solitary stretches of beach trying to get my bearings. Oblivious of time or the way in which the world was racing on without me, I watched long black ribbons of sea birds skim the waters. Perhaps the birds captured my attention because their movement mimicked my own. I was a woman skimming the surface of her life, a life suddenly rearranged and foreign. I understand today that grief was trying to transform me. I, that young woman in her twenties, was actually fighting to find a sense of life's power and reach and purpose; I was wrestling with life, not death. I was fighting for enough courage to withstand a force that had the appearance of total destruction . . . but that instead contained the seed of a vital awareness that was about to change me.

My books *Song for Sarah* and *Gift of the Red Bird* contain the earliest expressions of that new, emerging sight. As I fought my way through the unfamiliar landscape of grief, my heart eventually opened to a beauty and power different from anything I'd ever known. I saw that death was not the only challenge in front of me. The greater challenge was facing my illusions about life (the way I thought life *should* be) and my fear of change. I began to see that the great suffering that began with the death of my family was not solely because an accident had taken them away from me. I was suffering because I was in the grip of a system of beliefs that dictated how I understood love, how I faced death, and what I dared believe about life's meaning. Without my being aware of it, I had decided that certain conditions were essential for me to be happy. It was so subtle. Yet this series of quiet, inner beliefs were commanding everything about me. I had decided how both life and love *should* look. Now, in the face of loss, my inner demands were exposed. They, and not my circumstances, were my prison.

"Argue for your limitations," Richard Bach wrote, "and they are yours." I had been arguing passionately without knowing it. I never experienced my attitudes and opinions about life as argument *or* resistance. I called them *the way things ought to be*, or simply, *what I need in order to be happy.* Then an overwhelming grief jolted me, and the limits I'd put on life were there to be reckoned with.

Pain slowly began to crumble my defenses. New questions began emerging. Why was I relating to life by clinging to ideas and to people? Did I believe that my daughter was mine? Was I *really* entitled to her, or to anything? And if she and my husband were all that made life acceptable or meaningful to me, had they inadvertently become my god? What part of me was so rigid and demanding? I suddenly felt like a child: if life doesn't go exactly the way I say, I'll take my marbles and go home. Was this the best I could summon? Was there anything larger in me? Where was love?

I sat with the pain and began to listen. It took everything in me not to run away.

In time, a small measure of professional success followed the intense loss and upheaval. The worn journal where I recorded my pain, my questions, and my search for new understanding became a best-selling book, *Song for Sarah*. Thousands would eventually share both the story of my battle with grief and loss and my hard-won faith born from those hours. As I recorded my feelings across the pages of my journal, the hint of a greater design, a larger story embracing my particular story, emerged. That greater story became a light. It was a force powerful enough to penetrate the darkness. It moved me from my own circumstances to the dynamic of pain in all our lives. The compassion born in those hours became new sight: I wasn't alone.

Only the geography and the particulars of my situation were uniquely mine. The breaking of the human heart and the force of fear that I felt...the stubborn resistance to letting loss show me something I didn't yet know...the inclination to buckle under the pain...the seeming injustice of it all and the anger it created...the exhaustion that made me want to check out rather than go within and dig deeper, fighting the despair...the effort not to give in to self-pity, to put one foot in front of another and get past the seduction of seeing myself as a victim...all of these pressures and feelings were not mine alone. They are common to us all.

With my heart broken, I fed a newborn child and cleaned my home. Searing pain moved through me, screaming at me to attend to its presence, and still I kept living my life, day by day. I painted decks and baked cookies. I lived through months that seemed pointless and without redemption. The healing was not extraordinary or amazing. It was won in inches. Alone at night, I cried out to the universe: *What is the meaning of this? Of my life?* There were no immediate answers.

There were no audiences when I paced the floor at midnight...and at dawn...and at midday. I was not writing a book then. I was a woman writing in her journal, fighting to endure. I was someone learning how elusive courage can be. I was up against everything in me...my fears, my insecurities, my weaknesses. It was intensely private and amazingly universal. In those hours, although I didn't know it then, I was living in silent communion with every other human heart broken by sorrow. And one day I would stand before audiences in prisons and shelters...in finely appointed retreat centers...in hotel ballrooms...and I'd have something to say that mattered because of those nights of searing apprenticeship with pain. I would find my way because I refused to move away from grief until the pain did its work...until I was desperate enough to surrender old ways of seeing and let a greater love and beauty break through. The moment I decided to let go and allow grief to teach me, darkness began to reveal its hidden light.

But none of this was accomplished alone.

Slowly, one by one, a community began to appear in my life, a very colorful communion of saints. They arranged themselves in front of me, a strong, loyal chorus of support. They were educated and uneducated. Young and old. Knowledgeable and naïve. But every one of them rich in love. That was the key. They wanted to save me from drowning. They themselves didn't need to supply answers to the questions I was asking, nor did they have to be wise and beyond fear themselves. They didn't even have to know the way. The magic was love. They said, without using words, that the soul has company on this path. They caught my hand and held it.

Some sat with me, silently, in the dark. By their presence they encircled my life in their arms and said, *You're not alone.* I was often angry, dismissive, even rude, and they didn't leave. Day after day they showed up, in spite of me. They brought custards and cookies. They handed me books that might help and brought me beautiful nightwear and pieces of jewelry. They taught me how to knit and do crewelwork, activities that busied the hands but blessedly didn't require my mind. They endured my silences and my halting words. A community of souls: a living testament to my thin hope that healing was possible and that each life, even mine, was intended to embrace more than one dream. They helped me imagine that we were really intended to know joy.

Months into the journey with grief I found some words printed in an obscure literary bulletin. "We hear the rain, but not the snow...." I want to thank Kent Nerburn for being part of my community. I want him to know that upon reading those words, a power rose up in me. The words found their way into my heart. They challenged me to reach toward life with passion and intensity, to live so carefully that I would be aware of the sound of snow.

Was grief really so capricious that healing could be kindled even by a simple phrase? Apparently. Without any understanding of why those words moved me, I found in them a shimmer of light. That day, for the first time in months, I wasn't fully dominated by either anger or depression. I had crossed some imaginary inner threshold and found a willingness, at least in that moment, to open my heart again. I was willing because I wanted something. I wanted to know what it would be like to hear the snow. I wanted to experience a life that could be that brilliant. Anne Wilson Schaef said, "Choosing not to die is not the same as choosing to live." She's right. Now I found myself no longer satisfied with being half-asleep and half-awake. I wanted to be fully alive.

Ultimately the road of grief became a great opening through which a mysterious alchemy took place. My tears began to transform into courage. I was no longer hesitant to ask any question, and even to question the status quo. Pain began to shift into sight: I found myself thinking, *Maybe love appears in endless form, not just in one or two individuals to whom I cling. Maybe that's the point. Maybe we should be drunk with love all the time.*

Thirty years later, the thought of being drunk with love still speaks to me. Today I stand on stages and talk about the human journey, emphasizing all that is possible, knowing that the pain that once defeated me, the pain that was changed by love, makes this possible. The clarity brought by loss continues to teach

me, even after so many years. Once I became willing to learn, a new world opened, and it was a world I
hadn't seen before. Past my angry, passionate feelings
about life's injustices, something else was waiting to be
known. This new perspective was limitless. It encom-
passed the force of love and the greater nature hidden
within each person . . . a nature that feeds on freedom,
not fear.

> You cannot see the storms from
> the outside; they are carried on
> the *inside.*
> —Alison Asher

Subsequent deaths and losses, like my mother's
death, continue the process of learning and growth.
And each time, even if it is just one person, a community appears. It is seldom the same ones who helped
me in the past, because I've moved on, literally and fig-
uratively. Yet other beautiful souls come forward and
form the safety net of love that supports me on the
way. Perhaps no single act is more consequential than
reaching out to such a community and staying open
to the healing love it offers.

Sometimes I don't meet this community in person.
The love may arrive as a book placed in my hands
or the lyrics to a song. Still, it is the same. It is love

reaching out to encourage the emergence of greater love. That's the formula. It reminds me of times when I've looked up into the skies and found a particularly bright constellation, a pattern of light shining without expectation or demand. A glow of stars that is simply there. And I know that unconditional love, reaching out heart to heart, is like that bridge of stars.

Grief and Love

DURING THE FIRST MONTHS following the death of my husband and child, I locked myself inside my apartment. When the phone rang, I stared at the receiver until it was still. Friends knocked at my door, calling my name, and I wouldn't answer. If my arms could not hold the ones for whom I longed, then I wanted them empty. It was my angry choice, and my private choice. Hard barriers rose up inside me. In subtle, secret ways I had begun to say no to all of life because part of life had hurt me.

But my friends would not be turned away by my resistance. Their love persisted. To my chagrin they were not seduced by my "public" face, the one designed to convince everyone that I was fine. Nor were they put off by my refusal to answer the phone or join in common activities. Gently they kept chipping their way into my life, demanding that I know they were there. They pushed past the shadows where I wanted to hide and refused to accept the memory-filled half-life I was choosing. But they did so not by reprimand or judgment; they challenged me by loving me. They stubbornly clung to their vision of who I was and who they believed I *could* be, even following such heartache. They did what I could not do for myself in my broken state: they held onto the belief that I would heal.

Over a period of time, their love for me gained ground. It was a strong, silent intention that I remember how to love life back, and it forced me to choose between two strong forces — my memories and the fearsome, rough road of loving again. No one grieves without facing that choice. It isn't that we *can't* love again; it's that we *won't*.

Every Grief Is Unique

I WAS SOMEONE who withdrew, read a lot, and hungered for privacy as I wrestled with grief. I often felt angry, hurt, and betrayed, but I didn't want to show it. I wanted everyone to think I was doing well. It was the same way I tried to live my life. I, like most persons, was grieving congruent with my individual nature. Because of this, no two people, no matter how close, even if they are grieving the same loss, ever grieve in exactly the same way or at the same pace. Every grief and every griever is unique. We grieve as we live.

The strong, silent man or woman will not easily speak of his or her pain. A sensitive, emotional individual will weep with heartbreaking sobs. Introverts will keep their own counsel, possibly writing in journals, searching within for meaning. The extrovert will need an audience before whom to pour out the rush of words, and may not want to be alone at all. The person who has coped with life by *doing* will want to keep doing — fill up her schedule, get back to work, plan a trip — anything not to be left alone with the painful feelings. In grief we do not suddenly become someone new; we continue to be who we already are. Sometimes, in the initial impact of loss and pain, someone who is normally unexpressive *does* temporarily become emotionally expressive. This can be a great gift. But generally, for the long haul of the grief, people will revert to type.

The elderly and the young grieve differently. Spouses grieve differently. Two siblings grieving the death of a parent will grieve in ways unique to each of them. Men and women grieve differently. Parents who lose a child suffer the loss in individual ways. The same person grieves successive deaths differently. For instance, the loss of my mother, although powerful, did not affect me the same way that the loss of my spouse or my daughter affected me when I was only twenty-seven years old. Each grief represented a different relationship, grieved at a different period of my life. As we change (and hopefully deepen and grow) through life experiences, our response to grief also changes.

Grief is colored by our emotional nature, the time of life when we grieve a loss, and the special nature of our relationship with the one who died. The loss of a parent by a young child or teenager is experienced differently from the same loss for a grown man or woman who is fully established and surrounded by their own children, or who has satisfying work and a larger community. A grown child who never married and has remained closely allied with a deceased parent faces yet another set of circumstances.

Grief is also affected by the way grief was expressed (or repressed) in our families of origin and by what our culture tells us is "normal" or acceptable. A simple awareness that someone has lost a spouse, a friend, or a child does not tell the story. It is the *meaning* this relationship had for them that matters, and that meaning encompasses the bereaved's emotional nature, age, unique history of loss or injustice, their larger view of life . . . and whether or not they have developed a spirituality that sustains them. Intellectual beliefs alone do not support someone in the face of crushing loss and shattering illusions. They simply provide a framework for ways to think about loss. For instance, intellectual understanding may create awareness that loss is part of life, or that many throughout history have rebuilt and been *strengthened* in spite of defeat. Similarly, knowledge of the nature and stages of grief may facilitate understanding of the bereaved's intense feelings and reactions.) But the fabric great enough to support a transformation of pain must be able to touch the heart and soul as well as the mind.

You may experience many faces of grief or notice a variety of behaviors in someone close to you. Grief may:

+ provoke tears

+ turn to anger

+ manifest as an eagerness and a compulsion to talk

+ show itself by stony silence and a refusal even to mention the deceased's name

+ create a desperate need to control something else when the loss has left the bereaved feeling powerless

+ look like a determined busyness, which guarantees that there will be no time to be alone or to think and feel

+ appear as withdrawal and an unwillingness to draw close to anyone

+ become an overwhelming need to be held or touched

+ express itself as complete lack of interest in sexuality or intimacy

- lead to a dedication to a cause left unfinished by the deceased, or reading what they read, or pursuing their interests
- be felt as total inertia and the inability to initiate or participate in anything for a long, long while
- inspire impassioned devotion to causes related to the loved one's death (e.g., creating and promoting scholarships, memorials, legislative changes, or medical research in the loved one's name)
- result in a great desire for revenge or the need for justice

And, most confusing of all, grief may cycle its way through many or all of these responses, or seem to be many of them at the same time.

In the end, there are only two certainties: losing something or someone dear to us evokes feelings of sadness, and the healing process begins when the heart reopens to love.

Judy, a mother in Saskatoon, Canada, wrote this after losing her young son:

> If I had one request to make of those who came to be with us after our son was killed, it would have been to ask them to let us grieve our way. When six-year-old Danny died in a farm accident, my husband and I immediately acted out the roles that came naturally for us. While he huddled in a chair in shock and pain, I showed strength in

front of others. While he was either lost in another world or shaking with sobs, I appeared dry-eyed. We did this not by choice, but as the result of our individual natures.

Others were uncomfortable with our coping methods. At first I needed time alone to walk, think, and cry. I wasn't allowed that. Later when I wanted to talk about Danny, most people sat quietly, waiting for a chance to change the subject.

My husband also needed to be allowed to feel pain and cry. When he was overcome by tears, he was fed strong Valium by a friend. The day of the funeral he was told, "You've got to pull yourself together." That same day another person said to me, "You better not have too many of those pills," and refused to believe that I hadn't had any. My husband wasn't supposed to cry. I wasn't crying enough.

However, it wasn't long before our social conditioning molded us into acceptable people with appropriate coping strategies. I cope now by talking with friends, sharing my grief with those who are willing to cry with me. My husband acts the way a man is supposed to act. He talks to no one. He doesn't cry. While I have spent hard months and years crying and talking and working through my pain, my husband is trapped within his grief. And I could weep at that terrible injustice.

Many bereaved people will identify with (or at least understand) this grieving woman and her husband. Because relatives and friends often don't know how to act or what to say, their discomfort results in a desire to fix the bereaved friend's symptoms or prompts them to criticize the way in which grief is being expressed. The truth is that we all express grief in the only way we can.

Depression —
Part of the Grief Process

I OFTEN receive phone calls from anxious friends or family members expressing concern that a bereaved friend is crying all the time or is terribly depressed since an experience of loss. Inevitably the caller will add that the friend clearly needs help. Their tone implies that the grief causing this upset is two or three years old. But when I ask how long it has been since the loss occurred, it is usually fairly recent. And then I know who needs the help: the family and friends!

Depression is a very real and natural part of the grief process. Literally, the body is weeping and try-ing to heal. Just as a bird that flies into a windowpane is stunned, sometimes sitting still on the ground long after impact in order to regain equilibrium, those who grieve are adjusting to a mighty force that may have shaken them to the core. Even understanding this, it is nevertheless alarming to see a formerly vibrant, positive person shrink into a cocoon. So friends and family feel impelled to act, fearing that unless they force a change, the new, uncharacteristic behavior will become a permanent state.

The state of depression *is* new for many who grieve, but in healthy grief it will not be permanent. Like the frightened bird, the bereaved may sit still for a while, trying to recover purpose and direction. They may hover in their most familiar surroundings, soaking in the comfort of the few things that haven't changed. They are hunkering down in order to allow this phase of grief to pass. It is the emotional body's version of the bird's wisdom.

In recent history, following the horror of the terrorist attacks on September 11, 2001, the cities of New York and Washington, D.C., indeed the whole nation, exhibited a collective, stunned response. Few people ventured out to restaurants, movies, or theaters. Sports events were canceled; comedians fell silent. We all instinctively moved toward the comfort of home and community. Everyone slowed down. People watched and listened, trying to take in and absorb a reality for which we had no words. Most individuals felt aimless, unable to focus on work, sleeping fitfully, staring into space — depressed.

I remember standing on the deck at the back of my home in the Texas hill country on the morning of September 12. Dozens of hawks and buzzards were circling in the sky overhead. And suddenly I realized that this might be the only stretch of days in my lifetime when only birds filled the sky. (All air traffic had been temporarily suspended.) It was a deeply comforting thought. It reconnected me with the deepest root of things. It said that in the midst of chaos, birds were still flying. Nature prevailed. The assurance of that knowledge was immeasurable. Our nation had been shaken, but something greater than that moment carried on. In one way or another, all who grieve are searching for a mooring. *What doesn't change? Is anything constant?* Grief calls us to slow down and allow the sadness to pass through so a deep-rootedness may be found. It is not productive to engage in pointless activity or to be sedated during this time. When grieving, it's important to stop and be still so our hearts can find the bedrock.

How can you help when someone you love is reeling from such an impact? By recognizing depression as a stage and understanding that it is normal to be depressed following the pain of loss. The greater and more significant the loss, the greater the sadness.

Four months after the loss of my family I made this entry in my journal:

Everyone is so anxious for me to get better. They don't want me to hurt. But I do hurt, and I need

to cry. If I put on a brave face, it only helps them.
It drains me.

As grief progresses the bereaved may experience bouts of deep, uncontrollable crying, as well as a feeling that they are living on an emotional roller coaster. No one learns to love and depend upon someone else quickly, nor do we let go of deep attachments with speed. Healing takes time, and sadness and depression are part of the healing process.

However, if the crying and sadness create an ongoing state in which a person is more than sad and can no longer function normally, such as take care of themselves or their children, if they are not eating, sleeping...if there are no breaks between the darkest throes of pain, then professional help is warranted. If in doubt, always err on the side of safety.

Don't Rush Me...
Accept My Timetable

GRIEF IS A PROCESS, not a competition, and when friends and family convey patience and understanding with the process, the atmosphere for healing is greatly advanced.

Memories of my own earliest months of grief are still vivid. When the caskets of my young husband and small daughter were lowered into the ground, I was hanging onto sanity by a thread. No one was sure how to help me, least of all me. Coping with the enormity of my losses strained me to my limit. But I was also sensitive to the discomfort my circumstances created for those around me. I knew life would be easier for everyone if this accident hadn't changed our lives. Three months pregnant, my body simultaneously healing from both physical and emotional injuries, I knew my needs were overwhelming. My life was overwhelming. It overwhelmed *me*. But no force of will on my part changed what I was feeling inside.

As the weeks passed, my impatience to heal was fueled by the impatience of others. I kept telling myself that I had to hurry. I needed to be well again. I needed to return to "normal," whatever that meant. I judged myself unrelentingly, telling myself that others who'd faced my circumstances had healed more quickly or behaved more courageously. Even with my life in pieces, the harsh inner critic was there, telling me that brighter, more mature individuals would cope with the disaster more effectively. *It's taking me too long.* That was the summation of the greatest criticism I leveled at myself.

Inside, I was tense and raw — fighting just to make it through the hours. And then a well-meaning friend might say, *"By now you should be...,"* and I wanted to scream out loud.

By now you should be doing a little better...

By now you should be dating again...

By now you should be taking off your wedding rings...

By now you should be thinking about returning to work...

By now you should be getting rid of those clothes, putting those pictures away...

By now...

Without exception, those phrases were said to me, every single one of them, before I was ready to do what the speaker was suggesting. I used to think angrily, *How do you know? How can you know what is true for me when I can't even sort out how I'm feeling inside? If I don't know, how can you?*

Thirty years later, I have heard hundreds of bereaved persons echo that same frustration: friends or family members are ready for them to be healed and indicate their impatience by telling them what they ought to be doing or feeling, long before they are ready. The wish for the bereaved's life to "return to normal" exerts an extra pressure during an already demanding and difficult time.

Those who grieve need others to support their unique timetable. And as that friend, if you communicate your acceptance of whatever the bereaved is feeling, accepting the progress he or she has been able to make, you bestow a great gift. Criticism is always wounding; with grieving, it has twice the sting.

I learned that it isn't against the law to begin dating soon after the loss of a spouse, nor is it illegal *not* to be dating after being widowed for over a year. Or two years. Or three. A person will not be arrested for leaving the deceased's clothing hanging in a closet. Nor is it punishable to continue making regular trips to the cemetery for weeks, months, or years. Whether we admit it or not, most bereaved people have a cache of treasured items they choose to keep or a ritual they don't want to abandon for a long while. As long as there are other good signs (even minimal ones) of health, growth, and healing, those ties should not be judged.

Comments that began *"By now you should be..."* left me feeling worse about myself than I was already feeling. At the very moment when my life was turned upside down, those words seemed to measure me against some impersonal standard and implied that I could do better. They created a strong pressure, pushing me to grieve in an approved time and way so others would feel comfortable. But I simply couldn't schedule my grief.

My friend Glenna taught me a great deal about how my need to please others made me especially susceptible to the comments that advised me to hurry my grief along. One day she asked me directly what difference it would make if I *did* fulfill the outward signs of progress that seemed so important to everyone else. It was a revealing question. I saw that even if I forced myself to behave in a way that encouraged or satisfied others, I would still only be as far along on the *inside* as I truly was. I could make myself appear to be many things, but I couldn't change the reality that grief is an individual process, not a fifty-yard dash. Following our conversation I began to be more loving toward myself and more honest with others. This change, prompted by grief, became one that I maintained in my life. Pleasing people serves no one. Honesty is the real power.

When you grieve, learn to be accepting of yourself. Measure your progress only by examining your own growth, not by comparing yourself to anyone else.

As a friend, accept those who grieve *just as they are and where they are in the process.* Encourage them to be patient with themselves and gently remind them of the progress they have already made. Glenna's loving acceptance of me as I was, and where I was, moved me further forward in my healing than countless other remarks that were intended to hurry me along. Acceptance coupled with love became a powerful force.

Something to think about...

Whose timetable are you following in the grief process,
yours or your friends' or
family's? Even if others are
attempting to rush you or
judge you, can you remain
loving to yourself?

Embracing the Storm

✍ GRIEF WORK can be avoided initially. But not
forever. Eventually grief has its due. If grief is re-
sisted and not faced head-on, it goes underground but
often manifests itself as physical or emotional symptoms, sometimes developing into chronic bitterness or
resentment. These consequences are reason enough
to face grief directly. But suppressing grief is unwise
for another important reason: the grief itself contains
the seed for healing. Only through embracing brokenness, never in avoiding it or running away, is healing
found. Heartache, loneliness, and broken dreams are
powerful teachers. They cause us to ask the questions
that will point the way. *How am I relating to my life?
What matters to me? What lasts, and what doesn't? Is
there courage within me that I can summon?*

It is also compelling to resist grief because the grieving process is painful and because it leads us into uncharted territory. The bereaved often describe feeling as if they have been taken to a strange land. Everything on the outside is different and new, but even more unsettling is the fact that everything on the *inside* is also unrecognizable. One moment life seemed predictable; now it will never be the same.

If those who grieve feel bewildered by their new reality, it is understandable that friends and family will also feel discomforted. And if caring friends have no prior experience with deep heartache, if they have always been in control and have never felt lost, they may feel very unsure about how to help. Grief demands that the bereaved as well as their friends make adaptations and adjustments, learning to embrace newness and uncertainty.

For the majority of those who grieve, the first year of grief is all-encompassing, and the first experiences of facing holidays, anniversaries, birthdays, and so on force sizable adjustments and painful remembrances. A year ago the loved one was present. Now life's celebrations must be faced in his or her absence.

Grief is accentuated when basic life skills must be acquired. Many widowers have never lived alone, cooked, or shopped. Both men and women may be uneasy about staying alone at night, and they often sleep poorly. Some bereaved seniors have no license

to drive and are now alone with no means of transportation. It cannot be understated how difficult it is to
take on the challenge of new skills and living habits
when you are already overcome with sadness and feel
like a stranger living in a foreign land. Parents whose
lives have been totally oriented around a school-age
child are challenged with re-creating a daily rhythm
and routine apart from the school calendar that once
dictated the family's schedule. Parents of infants are
faced with filling hours formerly devoted to a schedule
of feedings. Those used to caring for an elderly spouse
or parent now have a freedom that seems hollow. In
every situation there is an experience of emptiness.
An empty house. Empty arms. An empty heart.

People manage the first days, months, and years
in various ways, because each individual brings her
own family history and emotional nature to the grieving process. Some individuals will initially appear to be
very much in control. Throughout the mourning rituals, and in the first weeks or months that follow, they
may appear unchanged. But appearances are not always an accurate picture of inner realities. Unusual
composure may not mean that death has been accepted, but rather may be masking the fact that the
bereaved isn't yet ready to face the enormous new
reality of loss. It is still too large to be taken in. In time,
as the bereaved is ready, he or she will begin a process
of incorporating the new reality.

When a loved one dies after a prolonged illness, the bereaved may have done significant "preparatory" grief work before the death itself occurs. Under these circumstances, the grief work that follows death is often shortened and less intense. The sharpest blow of grief may well have come when the terminal diagnosis was given. Succeeding months or years of caregiving have already offered the opportunity to grieve . . . especially to grieve the impending death together. Seeing a loved one in prolonged pain often softens the sting of death by triggering a desire for the loved one to be released from suffering. When this is so, death is greeted with relief, not with fear or despair. Even so, the actual moment when death is pronounced always carries a certain power. Even when anticipating death, we never think it will happen *this* moment or on *this* day.

Shock

EXCEPT IN CRITICAL SITUATIONS where professional help is obviously demanded (for example, if the bereaved shows the inability to function or is in danger of suicide), the shock of grief will wear away in its own time. Soon the bereaved will begin to feel and exhibit the effects of loss. But in the meantime, an immediate refusal to feel the loss is simply the body's way of coping. He is taking in as much reality as he can. If you want to help, let shock do its work. Accept him right where he is. Don't demand that your friend "face the facts." If he could, he would. And in time he will.

Some persons who grieve immediately weep and fall apart emotionally, sobbing through the rituals someone else attends with great poise. But after a time they may become emotionally spent and begin to feel a delayed, frozen calm. In whatever rhythm grief occurs, its impact is consuming, and the bereaved have little control over the waves of emotion or pain. Like a wild, raging fire, grief has its way.

In the first days following my own losses, I remember behaving with great control. I was dry-eyed through the funeral. I even wrote the eulogy. In greeting others, I remembered those who were celebrating birthdays and anniversaries. From all outward appearances, I was a sea of restraint and calm.

Yet I know how I behaved during that time only because others have told me. I cannot remember any of the particulars. Those events are either a blur or are totally blank. It was my state of shock, not my own strength, that allowed me to handle everything with such poise. Shock got me through the hours and the rituals. But inside of me was a great void. What looked like strength to others was a paper-thin façade. To me, nothing seemed real, and very little was registering. I was moving as if in a dream.

In three weeks' time, everything changed. By then I was reeling from the force of tears, washed over by anger, despair, and rage. When the assault of emotions began, I longed for the great void of the early days, but I could not re-create it. I was not in charge. Grief was moving, finding its mark in my heart, body, and soul.

What helps? Rather than debating whether or not your bereaved friend is in shock (and should or should not be), or whether she needs to face reality or gain control, it is much more fruitful to stand beside her as her inner storm rages and continue to be a source of love. Accept emptiness and tears equally, without judgment and with compassion, knowing that they are both part of the process of grief. If you care that she is hurting, the bereaved will sense it. Just open your heart. In grief, I fed on such love.

Also be sensitive to physical needs. My friend Susan remembers this well. Following the loss of her son Mark, she wrote to say, "Grief so assaults bodily functions, and for me, appetite was one. I was grateful that you never made a fuss trying to get me to eat, but rather, just left a couple of strawberries and a triangle of toast on a plate at the foot of my bed. Even that looked huge, but I usually managed to get some of it down. I will always use that as the gold standard for sensitivity.

"My friend Carolyn learned to just keep supplying me with a cup of hot lemon water and be sure my sweater was close by. COLD, so cold, for months. I later learned that hot lemon water is an energy balancer, but at the time I only knew that was what my body wanted. And Marcia bathed me. Made me get in the shower (she got it warm first) and scrubbed my back and washed my hair. Those are things I cherish."

Anger

TO SHARPEN YOUR ABILITY to love someone unconditionally, find someone who is grieving. The bereaved can be a challenge! To grieve is to live in the throes of great sweeps of emotion. You feel powerless in ways you never imagined, and feeling powerless produces fear. As the bereaved wrestle with fear, they are capable of sharpening their claws and striking back at anyone who is near. One minute you, the bereaved, might feel frustrated with your whole community, thinking that all human beings are insensitive and annoying. You wish everyone would stop calling and just leave you alone. The next hour you may be weeping because you feel so alone. Or you rail against friends and label them *insensitive.* You ask them to leave. Then five minutes later you long for them to return. The reality is that you cannot be pleased. Your behavior is driving everyone crazy, and it's driving *you* crazy too. You don't want to feel this way, but strong emotions are temporarily in charge. You'd like to say to people, *Please, love me as I go through this. I don't like it either.*

Before my family was killed, my busy life was blessed with friends whose presence enriched and delighted me. After Roy and Sarah's deaths, the same friends called and visited in great numbers, reaching out to me. But even though I sometimes wept because I felt abandoned and alone, I also found myself staring at a ringing phone without picking it up. Moving from my chair to the phone was beyond me. Talking was sometimes beyond me. The ringing phone might persist for hours as I stared at the wall, unmoving.

I also refused countless handwritten invitations. Or I accepted them, and then changed my mind at the last minute. Some friends became understandably angry and confused. And in that anger and confusion they became a perfect mirror of my inner landscape. I was in the constant grip of an inner storm that I couldn't control and didn't understand. I was angrier than I ever thought I could be. Life had dealt me a blow that seemed unreasonable, and my insides were revolting. I was angry with my husband and child for leaving me. It was irrelevant that they didn't have anything to do with choosing to go. This was feeling, not reason. I was angry with women whose spouses were still alive. I was angry with women who had spouses and complained about them, unaware of what they had. I was angry with families that were intact, when mine was not. I hated everyone who had what I'd lost. And then those very thoughts, difficult as they were, caused me to plummet one step further. They made me feel hateful toward myself. *What kind of a bitter person thinks such things? I reasoned. Look at yourself. You're a mess.* At any given moment those close to me felt the heat of these inner upheavals. I was a small brush fire.

What love it takes to see someone through such a storm. As a friend, you may find all your offers to help and your loving gestures dismissed, maybe even angrily. Your words and your reaching out may seem unappreciated. I'm certain you will sometimes want to flee. But please don't measure *your* worth by the responses of someone in pain. You are a lifeline in a storm, whether or not that is ever acknowledged. The value of your steadfastness is impossible to put into words.

None of those phone calls and invitations to me were wasted. Even when the calls went unanswered and the invitations were refused, the fact that my friends didn't walk away was vital to me. Anger might have held me in its grip, but the continuing gestures of my friends refused to let the anger have the final say. Every gesture of love said that in spite of an anger I couldn't control, I hadn't become unlovable. I wasn't hateful; I was in pain.

For the friend, walking with someone through these times is an exercise in love. To love someone who responds in kind is mutually rewarding. Loving someone who cannot summon a gracious response is difficult. But even when your efforts are met with a diminished response, or no response at all, press on. Such love has power.

Changes in Character

GRIEF ETCHES ITSELF deeply in the innermost parts and creates a great upheaval. It affects emotions, the spirit, and the body. As a result, those who grieve often change and seem "out of character." Yet, even knowing this, friends are surprised when the changes appear.

For many, grief provides the most powerful and important look, perhaps the *first* look, they have ever taken at life's deeper meaning. Those who grieve may be filled with questions. *Why is this happening? Why does loss occur for some and not others?* Grief rearranges priorities and introduces the bereaved to extremes of passion, anger, and sadness. It can be a reckless time of searing questions. Old conclusions may be seen in a new light. Real changes in outlook and behavior become possible in ways that didn't exist before.

For a period of time those who grieve may become uncommonly teachable. The force of the pain has shattered false assumptions and illusions, exposing them. The bereaved now know from experience that life is neither fair nor just, at least in the way society defines fairness and justice. It becomes clear that a love large enough to embrace death is different from romantic love. The result of these inner revolutions of thought and experience can produce a very welcome growth and healing. But it does not mean that friends and family welcome your new insights or the changes in your priorities and behavior. Human nature gravitates toward what is familiar, even if the familiar is restrictive. Feeling safe and secure is a strong impulse.

So if your bereaved friend suddenly stops living up to past expectations and behaviors — if they vary from past patterns... if they begin asking different questions or exhibit new priorities, it can strain present relationships. It is a common experience for a widow or widower to fall in love after the death of a spouse. Children, siblings, parents, even friends, may not initially meet the occasion with joy. Embracing change unsettles everyone. Sometimes a new mate or dating partner is difficult for others to embrace because it feels *too soon*. Sometimes he or she is seen as too radically different from the deceased. Yet in truth, the bereaved themselves are radically different, having passed over a threshold of pain and encountered the nearness of death to life. His or her new behavior may not be an indication of losing sense or control. The new behavior may be the very sign of *gaining* control over life, in some instances for the first time. Once a person finally understands the difference between passing worries and the legitimate, eternal matters of life and death, a new freedom becomes possible.

But for friends, whose lives have remained stable, and for whom there have not been great thresholds to cross, the new perspectives and priorities discovered by the bereaved may feel intimidating. Some friends want everything to stay the same. This tension may result in the bereaved finding new friends and developing new circles of acquaintances. The advantage of new friends is that they are not associated with the loss, have no common past, bring no expectations, and are unable to draw comparisons. They provide effortless acceptance. New friends accept you right where you are because they never knew you any other way.

When Close Friends Are Pushed Away

JIM AND BETSY were among the close circle of friends with whom my late husband and I socialized the most. Our families celebrated many occasions together, and our children played together. But after Roy and Sarah were killed, I refused most of their early invitations to get together. I couldn't have put my reason into words at the time because I didn't understand it then. My response seemed irrational, but it was strong. I started developing new friendships and let new people become my intimates.

About a year into my grief I offered to pick up an item at Jim and Betsy's home that a friend needed. I drove into their driveway without much thought, but the moment I stood in front of their door I doubled up with tears. It was all clear to me then. This house and these dear people, head to toe, were memories of Sarah and Roy. I couldn't look at them and their children, nor be in their home, without being flooded with what had once been mine. Everything evoked such strong memories of our two families being together, and in their presence there was no escape from the memories. To be with them was to be fully up against what I had lost. So I had instinctively avoided them. That's what I realized as I stood on their doorstep. My heart hadn't been able to manage the remembering, so

I had pulled back to ease my hurt. I chose other friends, newer friends, because they didn't evoke such remembrances. With new friends, there was an out...there was space for my mind to flee. I had avoided Jim and Betsy because they were the closest mirrors of everything that was gone. Being with them felt too painful.

But what love they held out to me. There may not be another phase of grief that requires more compassionate understanding. Even though my refusals to be with Jim and Betsy must have been hurtful and confusing, they never stopped inviting me to join them. They continued to include me. Their reaching out continued *in spite of* my responses. And eventually, when I was ready, I regathered them into my circle.

As I began to date, they extended invitations that included the different men I was seeing. Whether or not they silently wondered about some of my choices (I'm sure they must have!), their arms were open. When I moved from an apartment to a house, they helped me move. They watched me stumble through change after change in lifestyle and priorities with the words "We're right behind you." If they cringed at some of my mishaps, I never guessed it from their behavior. They grew with me. In accepting the timetable of my grief, they accepted me. My daughter Beth, born six months following the accident, was a bridesmaid in their oldest daughter's wedding. Their family was there when Beth graduated from college. And they reconnected with Beth on the East Coast, all of them, when she was in her late twenties. The love was strong enough to include that hard season of grief and endure beyond it.

It's difficult to put definition to such love, and yet it's the prized quality for which the bereaved long: someone who continues to believe in you while you find your way. Someone undeterred by your pain and the response it creates, continuing to be there regardless. Someone who stands by you *through thick and thin.* What a gift to have friends or family members willing to stretch in their own lives, who will resist the temptation to continually measure you against the person you "used to be." Jim and Betsy understood that I would not return to *normal,* whatever that meant. I was the person I had once been, plus this experience of deep loss and disorientation, and then the person who would emerge in the months and years ahead. Grief always picks a person up in one place and puts her down in another.

Strain between close friends is not usually permanent, and understanding the dynamics the bereaved are facing helps friends comprehend what is happening. Friends need to remain watchful until the mending period begins, and they should resist the temptation to sever ties prematurely. It should also be noted that simply because friends have been close does not mean they are necessarily the ones who will be most skilled in talking with you and listening to you about your pain. (If the relationship was particularly close, the loss may also be sizeable for *them*.) Just because someone carpools with you or lives next door does not guarantee that being a good grief listener is his or her gift. This always seems surprising. But friends enter our lives at different times and for different reasons. Someone who fills one role may not easily fill another.

For the bereaved widow or widower, being in the company of the couple with whom they and their spouse were a close foursome can be a biting reminder that the foursome is now one fewer. (This seems to be less true for the elderly than for those who are younger.) Parents who have lost a child may find it impossible to face other families who have children of a comparable age or children who were friends of their own child. Couples who've lost a newborn may struggle when seeing pregnant women and new mothers. And couples who have recently miscarried may find their hopes too bruised and their wounds too tender to be with another couple whose pregnancy is intact. Each situation that forces the bereaved to look into the eye of all they've lost can feel unbearable. It takes time to confront such realities.

Some of my dearest, closest friends waited the longest for our ties to reknit. I didn't want it to be that way, but I couldn't push any faster past the pain and fear. I was doing the best I could.

So what can a close friend do? Probably very little but wait. Maintain contact, but understand that refusals to your invitations reflect your friend's pain, not his or her heart. Sometimes it's helpful for a widow or widower to see members of a couple separately. I was able to do that with some of my closer friends. I needed the friendships and both male and female companionship, but I couldn't face them together at first. Seeing them individually was less of a reminder that I was now alone, and it helped bridge the roughest period.

When a friend has lost a child, be sensitive about bringing your own children when you visit, especially if your child and the bereaved's child were playmates or friends. Ask first if your friend would appreciate seeing you alone. She may be grateful for your understanding. In the case of older children, for example the teenaged friends of a deceased adolescent, the presence of your child's friends may be a great comfort. There are simply no hard-and-fast rules.

Some friendships never knit together again in quite the same way. This requires a great acceptance of change all around, and an understanding that change does not erase the joy that was. Change is only a *moving on*. We learn it over and over again: the basic principle of life is change.

Moodiness

GRIEF MIGHT BE considered synonymous with changes in mood. One moment those who grieve are angry, the next depressed; one day they are hopeful and welcoming, then annoyed by every comment and intrusion. My own grief journal captured some of those feelings:

Tonight I laughed and seemed my old self, and it was the assurance everyone wanted that I'm "me" again. "It's over," they probably thought with relief. But I know my momentary laughter was not an end to my tears. It was only a respite. Tomorrow I may cry again, or be angry, or depressed, or see no hope. I fear my emotions because they fly me back and forth. It's so hard, but that's the way I am now. I wish others could share my laughter, but not draw conclusions because of it. I'll need them again tomorrow, without judgment, when the tears start all over again. I must be terrible to love.

Moods are grief's nature, and since the moods of grief are particularly strong and variable, don't let them be your measure of how your friend or family member is doing. Up and down is how she's doing, and how she *will* be doing for a long time. Just learn, as a friend, not to take the moodiness personally. It isn't about you. It's about pain.

Loving and helping someone in the throes of such changing emotions demands great understanding and patience. You need a firm resolve not to let your own feelings be hurt by the many swings in mood. I was often guilty of rudely turning away a friend on Monday whom I would long to be with on Tuesday. Never in my life, before or since, have I experienced such powerlessness over my moods. All my actions that seemed to be harshly directed toward others had nothing to do with them. They just happened to be walking through my life when my pain intensified or seemed unbearable.

I always feared sharing my fleeting "good" moods lest they be misunderstood. What if friends thought the pain was gone because we had shared one light moment? What if they decided I was healed when I was still hurting so? Those who suffer from clinical depression express the same sentiment. There was such a desire to have others understand that no mood was the final mood. My moods were wild and varying and in constant flux. That's what I wanted someone to know.

Ironically, it was probably even harder for *me* to accept the fleeting "good" moods when they came — the moments of levity or amusement. I chastised myself after experiencing most of my earliest moments of joy. *How dare I laugh again when Roy and Sarah aren't even alive? Could I forget so quickly? Am I that insensitive? Hadn't I really loved them?* It felt as if sadness was the only proper response to loss.

Eventually I could see that my continued sadness did nothing to preserve the brightness that had marked our lives together, nor did it reflect the goodness that had passed between us. In fact, if the coming together of our beautiful lives for a short time, but with such meaning, now created *only* sadness and a diminishment of love in me, what did that really say? I couldn't bear thinking that the sum total of our wonderful years together was my malingering sadness. What tribute was that? In time I fought hard to allow a deeper love to awaken in me, one that was a true tribute to all we had meant to one another. Because of knowing and loving Sarah and Roy, I wanted love to grow in me. Because of them, I wanted my life to be devoted to something it might never have touched otherwise. Because of them, I ultimately chose to live fully.

The Body's Response to Grief

IT WAS A GREAT SURPRISE to learn that grief was affecting me *physically* as well as emotionally. I was unprepared for the feeling that someone had hurled a cement block into my chest. I hurt. The pain in my chest was strong and undeniable. "*Broken heart is not just figurative language*," said my friend Lois. I know she is right.

Grief often results in difficulties in both sleeping and eating, which may develop as either insomnia or a desire to constantly sleep. It may also trigger fluctuations in weight and a heightened susceptibility to illness. The bereaved are sometimes more accident-prone, or they may feel cold all the time, regardless of the season. The one who grieves may experience gastrointestinal disturbances and muscle tension. Typically grief is a time of low energy reserves; in order to cope with the inner storm and feelings of pain, the body is constantly calling upon its energy reserves to do the inner work. But inner work is not visible, and therefore not obvious. In spite of the fact that a day spent managing pain can be equivalent to a day of hard manual labor, it's possible that nobody knows how demanding grief is. If the bereaved's inner woundedness could be represented by an outer symbol, he or she would appear in full body cast. There are many days when everything is hurting and compromised.

It helps to get extra rest and to avoid unnecessary fatigue. It is not a time to take on strenuous physical activity. This is not the moment to hike in the Andes or begin a crash diet in order to lose an extra twenty pounds. The body needs the energy it can usually spare just to manage daily matters. A short amount of regular daily exercise (fifteen minutes of walking or biking, for example) is good, and it may also help with insomnia and lagging energy levels. But the physical demand should not be great, or the purpose will be defeated. Basically, the body needs love and care.

It is also prudent to reduce any stresses that can possibly be avoided or postponed. Friends and family can reduce some of those stresses by taking on every-day chores, handling carpool duties, buying groceries, providing meals, or helping with legal matters, for instance. This may not *seem* meaningful for those who think "helping" means counseling or bringing spiritual solace. The bereaved know differently. Offers to take over mundane chores help make it possible for the bereaved to keep going. I remember my friend Susan standing in front of a kitchen cupboard following the death of her son. She stared blankly at cans and boxes . . . food supplies . . . and finally said, "I know that all these items, put together, create a meal. But I don't remember how to do it."

It is *not* helpful to offer drinks or drugs to the bereaved to "soften" the pain. The effect will only be temporary, and sooner or later reality will reappear. The only way to transform pain is to experience it, and a friend or family member can help facilitate the beginning of that journey. If the bereaved sees drinking or drugs as his or her only way to cope, step in and hold her accountable or urge her to seek professional help.

Something to think about...

What emotional or physical
reactions to grief can you
identify in your friend? What
challenges do you notice to
your old definitions of love?

A Community of Friends

FRIENDS FORM a vital network. But even the
closest friends can be tempted to remain at a distance when death occurs, because they feel awkward
about what to do or say. They may also stay away because of an unconscious fear that death is contagious.
*If I allow myself to witness how fragile life can be, then
I admit that the same uncontrollable circumstances
may occur in my life as well.* The result of such fear
is that with each passing day the staying away creates
a greater gulf.

Perhaps your most difficult task as a friend is not
to abandon the bereaved because of your own insecu-
rity. Stay and hurt with him. He needs your physical
presence. He needs to know you are there.

Before my own grief experience, when *I* was the
anxious friend, I often excused myself from visiting

those who grieved by telling myself that death was a private time for family members. I rationalized that my presence would be intrusive. Then *I* became the bereaved. And I learned that even though the bereaved do seek moments of privacy, they also wanted to know that those they loved were there. I remember to this day some of the people in my community in Connecticut, many of whom I knew only by sight, who walked through the receiving line at the memorial service held for Roy and Sarah. I was a relative newcomer to the community, and there were few people whom I knew well. As many persons spoke to me, my friend Jim stood beside me, helping me with names. People came, not because they knew me or my family well, but because they were part of my community. They came bearing love.

I also remember the confusion of grief. The fear. The hurt. Grief left me feeling like I was inhabiting a new land, but a land that existed deep within myself. I often wondered, "Will I ever be *me* again?" The inner newness made it doubly important to be surrounded by friends. They represented the things in my world that *were* known and familiar, which hadn't changed. Friends were my link. They reminded me of the stable order of daily life. Through their presence I felt comforted, and that gift was substantial.

Thoughts on Visiting

THE FIRST VISITS to the bereaved in the days immediately following loss provide an important link to the "usual" world. To your grieving friend, you are one part of the familiar structure that has not been ripped away. Every person who enters the bereaved's new reality is another step toward healing. So, again, don't stay away. But your visits needn't be (in fact, *shouldn't* be) long unless the bereaved specifically requests otherwise. Drop off your book or casserole, chat for a few minutes, and be on your way. A short visit tells someone that you care without invading her space or privacy or requiring large expenditures of energy that she simply doesn't have. In the early weeks of grief the bereaved's mind is racing nonstop with the reality of loss, and a heavy inner exhaustion permeates everything. *Brief* visits and phone calls are greatly appreciated. The enormous energy it takes for the bereaved to do the simplest things cannot be overstated. As time went on and I felt stronger and more open to having company, I often urged someone to stay longer. But it was much easier to say to someone, "Please stay a little longer," than it was to find the words to ask someone to leave.

Also think about the timing of your visit. The timing of a visit can be the visit's most important variable. Close friends want to be present for the roughest moments, but that coincidence happens only by chance. The roughest moments often occur in the middle of the night or on days when everyone is occupied. Still, there is a way to increase the likelihood that your ongoing visits will be beneficial.

Friends frequently decided to visit me on Sunday afternoon. It was wonderful to see everyone, but when five or six people arrived within the same period of time, I was unable to talk to any one person ... and sometimes I really wanted to. My friend Anne *asked* me when I'd like to be visited. I chose Tuesday evening, when my newborn was asleep and I was typically alone. Then, if I felt like talking, the hours were usable. Generally, think about visiting parents with young children at a time when the children aren't up, needing their attention. When young children are active, deeper conversations cannot take place. Also remember that Sunday evening can be one of the loneliest times of the week for those who grieve, especially widows and widowers. The new week is ahead, but forever changed for them. Every approaching Monday is a reminder that the world has moved. The key is this: time your visit to align with the bereaved's schedule and needs, not your own.

If your friend is part of a family, avoid arriving when other family members are home and you and she will have the least privacy. Conversely, when the bereaved lives alone, Sunday can be long and lonely, and a

day when a visit is particularly welcome. It only requires a little thought to arrive at the best time. It's also
helpful to ask the bereaved themselves when it's hardest for them to be alone, and most desirable to have
company; then you can orient your visits with greater
sensitivity.

Anne always called me on Tuesday evenings to see
if my new baby, Beth, was in bed. When the baby was
asleep, she arrived. Those evening hours were unin-
terrupted and private. If Anne had visited at four when
Beth was hungry, cranky, and needing my attention, I
could not have spoken to her freely about the things
that were filling my heart. The fact that she was willing
to fit her visits around my schedule spoke volumes to
me about her genuine caring.

Many Tuesday evenings Anne and I sewed together,
working on small projects. Sometimes we hardly
talked at all. Other evenings the handwork never got
picked up...the conversation was flowing. Regardless of how we spent those hours, it was an evening
for me to look forward to each week. And if I needed
or wanted to talk, the hours were truly usable.

Sorrow That Cannot Be "Fixed"

THE HUMAN HEART longs to alleviate suffering . . . our own, as well as the suffering of others. But if you have grieved deeply or been close to someone whose loss is great, you know that grief can neither be rushed nor "fixed." Few experiences defy control as staunchly as grief. Grief has to be gone through. In fact, it *must* be gone through. Experiencing the pain is a necessary step toward healing.

It is a great challenge to the human heart to offer companionship and compassion without being able to make things better. After visiting your bereaved friend you may feel disturbed or uncomfortable. You've become acutely aware of someone else's pain, but you are unable to erase it. It hurts to stand beside someone who is in pain and feel that your efforts to help have brought no benefit.

During the early weeks of grief, my cousin Nancy got sitters for her children and arranged to spend one day a week with me. At that time I wasn't thinking about anyone else's life. All I could cope with was the shock of my own circumstances. The loss was still so penetrating that I struggled to show much sociability. One afternoon Nancy put me in her car and drove to Newport, Rhode Island, to give me a change of scenery. I remember sitting numbly by the water feeling as if I were drowning, even though my feet were planted squarely on land.

What could it have felt like for Nancy? She was saddened by my pain and powerless to change it, yet time after time she came back to see me. There was absolutely nothing gratifying in those days for her; it was something she did for me in a pure spirit of love. I'm sure she doubted the effect of her gestures, and I doubt that I expressed much appreciation. But her standing by me meant more than she will ever know.

It can be challenging to love the bereaved. Friends reach out, sometimes receiving very little in return. They are witnesses to a pain they cannot remove. But in return, they learn mightily about love.

Alison Asher said it well: "Most painful errors can be avoided by simply asking ourselves one important question: 'Am I trying to fix it?' Even the most well-meaning gesture offered from a need to fix it will come across as intrusive.... The desire to fix someone else comes from our own personal fears.... Regardless of our deepest good intentions, if we contribute to others from a place of fear, we contribute more fear and anger to the situation."

The Power of Telling Your Story

IN THE MONTHS following my losses, I felt compelled to tell the story of my loss to anyone who would listen. I repeated the details surrounding my family's deaths over and over again. Sometimes I embarrassed myself by telling the story to virtual strangers, like a cashier at the grocery store or the person servicing my car. Yet the words seemed to have their own force, and in spite of myself, I told that story.

Eight years later my childhood neighbor, "Grandma" Wild, died. Following her death, whenever I visited the town where I grew up, I'd spend an hour or more in the evening sitting with her widowed spouse. And even though I'd come home for Grandma Wild's funeral (I delivered the eulogy), Grandpa Wild would begin each visit by retelling the events surrounding his wife's death, just as if I didn't know.

It's easy to attribute his behavior to advanced age and forgetfulness. Or even to conclude that he didn't yet fully understand what had happened. But since I had already walked that same road (and behaved in exactly the same way), I knew that neither was true. His telling the story had nothing to do with age or denial. Nor was it linked to any need to inform or remind others. *He repeated the story in order to believe it himself.* With every telling he came closer to accepting the unthinkable reality.

Telling the story is a mental trying-on. It's a process of taking an enormous reality and breaking it up into pieces small enough to fit inside of you. It's a way of taming something wild and unruly until it becomes manageable. It's an effort to help you believe that this really happened. It's a means of accepting a day and date after which nothing is ever the same.

The value of a friend who listens without judgment to the retelling of your story is inestimable. In effect, that action helps the bereaved confront his or her pain. You become what they need: a witness to their lives. There are no norms about how long this process takes. The story being told represents a painful reality. When that pain finally begins to be integrated, the telling stops. Even though the bereaved may still resist some of the changes death forces them to accept, the loss has begun to find its way into their being. Only then will they be able to move on to the next stage of the grief journey.

Bringing Up the Loved One's Name

ॐ FRIENDS CAN FEEL understandably timid when it comes to speaking about the person who has died. They question whether or not to share with you their own memories and personal feelings of loss. It's easy to conclude that if you are visiting someone in order to help (which somehow translates into "cheer"), then certainly it must be ill-advised to risk saddening them even more by bringing up painful memories.

But your bereaved friend is already sad, deeply sad — maybe sadder than he or she has ever been. And the fact that someone tries to distract them by avoiding any mention of the loss does not remove the sadness, not even for a moment. On the contrary, the mind of the newly bereaved does not shut off. The loss is relentlessly there, every waking hour. She cannot stop thinking of what has happened and all that has changed. And because of that, conversations that speak to the one topic her heart can hear are helpful, not harmful.

The sympathy notes and cards I treasured the most were filled with the sender's own recollections as well as with personal expressions of their own feelings of love and loss. Some of the conversations I remember most fondly were those in which friends talked with me about my husband and child, sharing their own memories. Through the eyes of others I was given new glimpses of my husband . . . as a teacher, friend, or nephew, for instance. And these gifts made me feel as if my "knowing" him wasn't over.

Sharing your own feelings and memories also says to the bereaved that the loss of this individual is significant to others as well. The person they loved matters. They are not experiencing a terrible sadness that no one else shares. Your speaking about the one who died says that a surrounding community remembers and cares. So speak about the deceased and say his or her name. The bereaved needs to hear that name. And don't rush to remove pictures and mementos from your home. The fact that you remember and value your own memories tells the bereaved that her loved one's life had meaning and won't be forgotten. Shared remembrances offer a great, sustaining strength.

Honest Conversation

UNTIL YOU EXPERIENCE deep loss firsthand, it's impossible to imagine the energy that grief requires. Grieving *is* work. And one of the greatest expenditures of energy in the initial weeks of grief is the energy required to make polite conversation. Energy drains every time you enter a social situation where you feel required to avoid speaking about the loss or to pretend that nothing has changed. This may help visitors, but surely not the bereaved. In fact, grief changes everything and everyone. After her child died, my friend Theresa wrote, "We are forever changed. My husband and I both feel robbed of our youth, innocence, and laughter."

I always dreaded meeting friends and acquaintances with whom my loss had not yet been acknowledged. I dreaded the encounters because so few people treated me honestly. If I'd been wearing a leg cast, they would have known how to respond to my injury with interest and concern. But I was wounded without any outward signs, and no one knew what to say to me.

Rather than address my loss, some friends and acquaintances avoided my eyes and initiated superficial conversations. Their discomfort was very clear. They didn't know what to say or do. My loss was like a hot coal, and no one wanted to touch it. I was already feeling awkward and changed, someone who no longer fit in. When I added to this an awareness that others could not speak to me honestly, it only intensified my heartache.

What I desperately needed was honesty. I didn't need my sorrow to be "unmentionable" or my friends to pretend nothing had changed. I needed someone to look into my eyes and say, *"I'm so sorry."* Only looking into the raw truth of things had the power to make a difference. I needed the grief to be spoken between my friends and me. One by one, I needed the world outside me to meet the new world within me, and I needed help to find a way to make the two worlds mesh.

To friends and family members, the words *I'm sorry* may seem inadequate and unhelpful. But the words are symbolic. It is the act of acknowledging the loss that matters, and any words that do so are like a bridge over a great chasm. How grateful I was for everyone who listened and offered simple words of love at that time in my life. They helped me find my way.

What do you talk about with someone who's grieving? You don't have to say anything. Acknowledge the loss, and then just listen. As the bereaved speak, they may connect with feelings that have been buried in their hearts for a long while. In talking about these feelings, the grief begins to shift. Tears, anger, writing, speaking, physical activity — all of these help grief to move. Some find that running and long-distance walking help to metabolize the grief. Grief *needs* to move. Feelings need to be repeatedly uncovered, accepted, and then let go. In the very process of naming and owning feelings, healing begins.

In the hours after a loving listener allowed me to talk, I was always relieved. It was as if I had been provided with a new supply of energy. Even though the conversation might have been immediately draining, even if it provoked tears, the net result was always renewed strength.

I knew quickly whether or not my visitors were comfortable enough with pain to really listen to me. Sometimes their open-ended statements alerted me to their readiness. They might say, *I can't imagine what this is like. Do you feel like talking about what's happening to you? Do you feel afraid?* Every statement of caring was my cue that someone was willing to navigate the hard feelings *with* me. If I felt like talking at that particular time, I could take those statements and create a deeper conversation. If it wasn't a day when I felt able to be verbal, I could offer simple responses that at least acknowledged the invitation to speak. I truly appreciated those who let themselves be guided by *my* cues, and not their own agenda.

Things Not to Say

SINCE EVERY grief and every griever is unique, it *is* hard to feel sure how to respond. There are no easy answers. But here are some guidelines.

Call me if you need me! These words are always said with love, and probably with the full intention of following through on a request if the bereaved does call. The words mean well. But, unfortunately, grief can be painfully paralyzing. Ten days following a burial or

cremation, when grief is breaking the heart, the bereaved may very sincerely want to talk with you ... but
the distance between that thought and the phone is
too great.

My friend Lois described this experience perfectly in
her grief journal: "Sometimes I feel that I am drowning,
too far from land to reach anything or anyone, unless
someone reaches out first."

The key to helping is that you, the friend, need to be
the initiator. Make the calls yourself, or simply show
up, offering to take a walk, go for a drive, have a cup
of tea. The specifics don't matter as long as your invitation is definite and sincere. The newly bereaved person
needs friends to reach out first.

You might say something like this: "I'm free at noon-
time tomorrow. Would you like to have lunch with
me?" Or, "How about seeing a movie together this
evening, or taking a walk tomorrow morning at ten?"
Once you've asked, let the bereaved be honest about
whether or not she feels like having company or going
out. A visitor can be powerful medicine, and it may be
wonderful to feel a friend's nearness for an hour. But
even if your offer is refused, know that your caring will
have mattered. Try again on another day. Be concrete,
and above all, don't give up on your friend.

If you are creative, you can come up with specific
ways to show your willingness to be available at any
time ... especially at those times when a wave of grief
has hit. One friend left me a card with her name and

number, and these words: *I want to be called in the middle of the night!! I have no children to care for, and I awaken easily.* I was touched by her effort to empha-size her availability and willingness to be called at an hour when I would surely hesitate to awaken a friend. If she had said, *Call me anytime,* I wouldn't have called in the middle of the night.

My friend Jan was especially sensitive to how it feels to be a single parent caring for a sick child. She re-peatedly stressed her understanding of what it must be like to be alone tending an ill child in the middle of the night, worried about croup or a high fever. "Please don't ever be alone and afraid in that way," she told me. "I would want to come and sit with you, even if I couldn't do more than lend moral support." Her concern was so specific that I felt free to call when a nighttime vigil became hard to face alone.

Something to think about...

How can you be more specific
in your offers to help?

It could have been worse! "You're lucky! It could have been worse! There are others in circumstances that are so much harder." What harsh, unfeeling words.

Unthinking words. Such phrases can make the bereaved volatile, because no one who is newly grieving feels fortunate.

I remember lying in the hospital following the accident in which my family was killed. A visitor appeared and said, "Oh, how fortunate that you lived! How wonderful that your pregnancy is intact. You are so lucky!" I wanted to shoot the person on sight.

Considering all conditions on this earth, and the breadth of a lifetime, I *am* lucky, and I do consider myself fortunate and richly blessed. Today, many years later, I am grateful I lived, and even more grateful that I was pregnant at the time and that the small fetus was hardy enough to survive. But in 1975 in the immediate days surrounding my loss, life was an indescribable nightmare and I was incapable of thanksgiving. The last thing I felt was *lucky*. All I felt was pain and a longing for friends to validate that pain, not belittle it. My broken heart cried out to be held and touched. It was that simple. My friend Susan remembers how vital touch was when her son Mark was killed. I was with her at the time, and another friend named Susan and I sat and held her in the hospital. One of us stroked her hands and face, another her feet. Years later, the touch and not our words is what she remembers.

There are always ample future days to consider a loss measured against a whole lifetime or against other human suffering. But in the early moments of hurt, those who grieve may not see beyond their present reality. Early grief is not magnanimous. It is the raw experience of pain, powerlessness, and fright. The griever needs to be consoled, not chided. Gratitude is something you reach on your own. Imposing it only hurts.

I know how you feel. . . . Meant to express oneness and compassion, the words *"I know how you feel"* usually trigger resentment. They cause friction because they carry so little truth, even if the speaker believes he has had an identical experience. In fact, we can never know the exact shape and experience of someone else's pain. Even when I speak with other grieving parents, I only "know" what it means to be hit with the impact of losing a child. I know the nature and horror of such an ordeal and what it unleashed for me. I know what it means to suffer deeply. I understand the level of shock produced by losing a child, as well as the great length of the healing journey. But *exactly* how it will be for another grieving parent? That I cannot know. It is so much better to say, *I can't imagine how hard this must be* or *I hurt because you hurt* than to say you know how someone is feeling.

In fact, it's not necessary to "know how someone feels" in order to minister to them well. It's only necessary to be loving and kindhearted, to listen and stay close. My friend Sandy was one of the most compassionate caregivers in my grief, yet she'd never lost a child or spouse. Her sympathy and understanding flowed from her humanity and from other experiences of loss. Those personal encounters with pain, though different from my own, opened her heart and guided her as she tenderly supported my broken heart with compassion.

Support groups are built on the principle that a special bonding occurs between those who have experienced similar losses. And this is true. But even then, every loss is unique, and the depth of grief is always individual.

Don't worry, you'll remarry. You're young; you can have other children. It may very well be true that the bereaved will one day choose another spouse or bear more children. But future possibilities do not soothe immediate pain. In fact, such words seem to dismiss it, denying the enormity of present circumstances by implying that one human being can handily replace another.

No sorrow over the loss of one child is removed by the arrival of another. If only that were possible! Having another child or finding a new heart to love may ease certain passages, but the original loss still must be grieved. The bereaved misses a particular person, someone they knew, touched, and loved — not a child, parent, or spouse *in general*. Human beings are not generic, and we cannot substitute one for another. The bereaved must grieve the one who is gone, and that need should not be diminished with suggestions that new persons to love can make the loss "feel better." There are no shortcuts. That may be the hardest lesson of all.

Asking "What If?"

WHEN LOSS OCCURS, those who grieve experience emotional, physical, and spiritual upheavals, all of which give rise to questions. The two words "what if" seem to form a common question for the bereaved. *What if I hadn't left his room for those few minutes? What if I'd been driving instead of her? What if I hadn't let her go to the party? What if we'd left just five minutes later, or three minutes earlier?*

In terms of actually changing reality, asking "What If?" is a futile exercise. There is no absolute control in life, and there is never any guarantee that different choices would have reversed a particular outcome. But in the earliest days following an accident or a sudden death, it is tempting to use hindsight and to believe that some action on your part *could have* or *would have* prevented the loss.

If the bereaved begins to wonder "What If?" in your presence, listen and offer love instead of "answers." Friends don't need to react by countering the bereaved's thoughts one by one. Answers aren't needed;

what matters is being able to voice the questions. What *might have been* is unknowable. When the bereaved is ready, she will accept what *did* happen. In the meantime, imagining other conclusions is an important step toward final acceptance. People ask *"What If?"* until they can accept *what was*. It's almost as if we must try on every other scenario imaginable before accepting the reality that is. It's a last attempt to change the unchangeable, if only in the mind. The final admission is that none of us have ultimate control.

Feelings of Guilt

AFTER LOSS, survivors review their relationship with the one who has died. Inevitably, because every human relationship has moments of disharmony and friction, he or she begins to experience feelings of regret and guilt. One person remembers times when he was cross or demanding. Another dwells on past mistakes. Someone else recalls moments of frustration and anger, asking himself if there was more he could have done. *Was I loving enough? Did I spend enough time with them? Were there signs I should have recognized earlier (e.g., hints of impending illness), steps I should have taken?* Survivors are tempted to berate themselves for not being perfect. It is a rare person who ever feels that they have done enough or been enough.

If your bereaved friend feels guilty and says so, let her talk about those feelings. Many bereaved feel responsible for the death, even when no reasonable circumstances support that conclusion. Some, like myself, simply feel guilt about being the survivor. It was a long while before I named that feeling inside me. It rose up while I was watching a movie in which a young man finally expresses his own guilt for living through an accident in which his brother drowned (*Ordinary People*). As I sat in the theater I realized that I too harbored a survivor's guilt. I walked outside taking deep breaths, letting the emotion wash over me. Naming and owning the feeling was a powerful key to my healing.

My initial question to the universe, *Why did they die?,* slowly became, *Why did I live?*

The guilt of living when someone you love has died is especially painful when grandparents experience the death of an infant or a young child. Since their own lives have been nearly fully lived (in fact, they may even be infirm and ready to die), it is particularly anguishing to watch a young life end prematurely. They may ask the question, *Why couldn't it have been me?*

Working through guilt means an ultimate acceptance of life's mystery and impartiality. It means forgiving yourself for not being perfect and accepting that each of us can only do the best we can at any given moment.

This well-known prayer comforts many who are torn by guilt:

> God grant me the serenity
> to accept the things I cannot change,
> the courage to change the things I can,
> and the wisdom to know the difference.
> — attributed to Reinhold Niebuhr

In the end, the past can never be changed. All we can change is how we live today.

God's Will?

THE HEART TORN by loss searches for explanations. It asks why life is unjust and unfair. Asking "Why?" can be both passionate and consuming. Having lost a daughter by suicide, my friend Priscilla wrote, "Why? is a cry of pain from the soul for which there is no answer." Yet those who grieve know that the cry is real.

Friends also desire to understand the loss. Because of this, numbers of well-intentioned friends rush in during the early weeks of grief to assure the bereaved that the loss was (or wasn't) God's will. In particular, the clergy often hope to sustain the bereaved by offering theological explanations. The plain truth is that there is no explanation that satisfies raw pain.

When I was given scriptures and verses in the early days of my grief, I wanted to shout, "I'm not ready!" First I needed to be free to hurt and, possibly, to be angry with God. I needed to be free to wrestle with all my prior beliefs and values, including who God was, and why horrible circumstances are permitted in our lives. I needed to weep and be human. I needed to ask "Why?" over and over again, long before I could consider answers to that question. I needed to embrace my brokenness before I could mend it.

When it was time to beg theology for answers, I searched on my own. I initiated months' worth of searching. But I didn't do that until I had first absorbed the chaos of my circumstances, and until I could believe that it had all really happened.

The clergy and friends who helped the most offered me the love of God, rather than imposing their own *beliefs* about God. This freed me to cope with God in my own time and in my own way. (Those who are already steeped in scripture and in a firmly rooted faith will of course lean *toward* that faith, rather than *from* it. But there are others, like me, whose younger faith may be shattered by profound loss.)

I ultimately concluded that just because God wasn't the God I had imagined or wanted (i.e., a God who prevented pain and tragedy), still, God was there. As I relaxed my narrow image of God, I became willing to ask, for the first time, who God truly was. I couldn't have borrowed that knowledge from anyone, no matter how much I trusted and respected them. I had to meet God myself, in my own dark night.

It may take a long while for the bereaved to sort through the questions provoked by theology. If they have never embraced a personal theology, the entire path is new. Even if they do have strong former conclusions, everything may come up for review. It consoled me to learn that the faith that arises from a deep personal search inspired by grief is often deeper and stronger than a faith that has never been questioned.

Each person finds his or her own answers concerning God's will. No one effectively borrows anyone else's conclusions. However long it takes, the bereaved search. The means to finding truth and peace is irrelevant; all that matters is the seeking.

Living with Questions

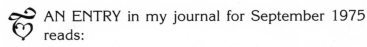 AN ENTRY in my journal for September 1975 reads:

My mind is filled with questions. I feel as if the questions have taken over the inside of me. I

wonder if they will drive me mad. Where are my loved ones now? Will Sarah grow up or remain twenty-two months old? Are she and Roy together? Do they miss me? Will I catch up with them one day, or will I always be left behind?

I reread that entry today, many years later, still able to remember the feelings of that young woman who needed answers so badly. I would have killed for answers then. But in the end, the most tormenting questions had no specific answers. There was no day of clarity or definite knowing. In the end, there was God. That was the answer.

God's presence eventually assured me that my loved ones are safe and well. Perhaps they are still learning, as I am learning. Perhaps they grow, as I do. Certainly, when we meet again, we will know one another in some way. I don't need to know more. I've made my peace with mystery.

The bereaved live with questions, doubts, and fear. They wrestle with the mystery of life and death. As a friend, listen to their anguish-filled thoughts, and support them in a search for greater knowledge. The power of deep questions leads many to know God intimately for the first time.

The Power of Prayer

LOOKING BACK ON MY OWN long journey through grief, I now realize that I was guided every step of the way — not by burning bushes or "a still, small voice" — but by God working through many means: through wonderful, sensitive friends, through insights, through the wisdom found in books, and through the tremendous opportunities that filled my path. I was eventually able to avail myself of the help friends offered and the teachings and opportunities life presented. Today it seems clear that this became possible because so many people were praying for me.

"I'll pray for you" is not an idle comment. Friends who said this to me actually fulfilled the commitment. And the insights and spirit generated by their prayers surrounded me and gave me every advantage to heal. I know that. I did not find my way alone.

In *The Last Thing We Talk About,* Joe Bayly wrote the following:

I was sitting, torn by grief. Someone came and talked to me of God's dealings, of why it happened, of hope beyond the grave. He talked constantly. He said things I knew were true. I was unmoved except to wish he'd go away. He finally did. Another came and sat beside me. He didn't talk. He didn't ask me leading questions. He just sat beside me for an hour or more, listened when I said something, answered briefly, prayed simply, left. I was moved. I was comforted. I hated to see him go.

Pray for those who grieve, because prayers generate power. Pray that your grieving friend will learn to transform pain into a new freedom . . . an experience of life's richness and beauty. Pray because every healed heart benefits the world.

Something to think about . . .

You cannot force your own answers on someone who is asking "What if?" or "Where is God?" But you aren't helpless. You can pray. Through prayer, both you and the bereaved are changed.

Specific Ways to Help

NOT EVERYONE who cares about someone who is grieving is close enough or comfortable enough to be the one who listens to grief's outpourings. But there are still considerable ways to help. Love comes in many forms.

How grateful I was to those who loved me by offering rides (to and from doctors' appointments, meetings, church, and so on), shopping for emergency grocery items or prescriptions when I couldn't get out at night with a new baby, or babysitting so I could change my scenery for a while. Friends invited me to play tennis, dropped off magazines they thought I would enjoy, left flowers to brighten my day, and offered to go with me to functions that were difficult to face or attend alone. In fact, one neighbor, Doug, saved my sanity the second Christmas after my loss by helping me put up a small tree. I had struggled unsuccessfully for hours to do it on my own, and my nerves and emotions were frayed. It took him fifteen minutes, and I've remembered that kindness for many years.

A man attending a talk I was giving on grief told me afterward that I had just validated the many brownies he had baked and brought to the bereaved over the years. He had always felt secretly ashamed that his "gift" to others did not include the skills of counseling and compassionate listening. I assured him that on some days there *was* no greater gift than chocolate.

In very unique ways, friends help the bereaved hold together the outside structure of his or her world. Both the inner and outer worlds need love and attention, and some of the most practical gestures are the most in-valuable. I remember joining several friends to wash windows and put up screens for an older widow in our church community. It was true that she also needed conversation and comforting, but it was no less true that the care of her windows was a huge worry. Having that taken care of, she could turn to her inner healing.

Run Errands

DON'T HESITATE to ask if there's a specific errand to be run or a handyman job to do that might be helpful. But understand that the friends who are easiest to call upon are those who are most definite about their willingness and availability.

For instance, I loved it when someone said, "I'm free on Thursday morning from nine to eleven, and I would like to do something for you then. Are there any handyman jobs to do?" Or, "I'd like to drive you to your next doctor's appointment. When is it scheduled so I can put it in my book?" When friends were that specific, I knew they really wanted to help and had the time to do so. By indicating some free hours or mornings, they erased my fear that I might ask for help at an inopportune time. I didn't want to impose on friends who might say yes to me (even when it was inconvenient for them) because of pity or guilt. If someone made a specific offer, I knew they were genuinely willing and available to help me.

Allow Reciprocal Favors

IN TIME, if your grieving friend offers, it's also important to let him or her reciprocate with a favor. When someone is only receiving help and never giving it, self-image lowers. So if the bereaved offers to help you, or asks questions about some of your own struggles, share a little. Even though she is hurting badly and may be more in need of support than you are at the moment, it's still important for her to feel that in some measure she can be a friend in return.

My own losses were so enormous in the eyes of my friends that anything they were facing at the time seemed insignificant in comparison. It took me a long while to convince them that heartache is heartache, whatever its size or source. I felt left out and even more isolated when friends didn't include me in their day-to-day complaints and mishaps. I'd been robbed of so much. I didn't want to be robbed of the chance to be a good friend as well. And I needed to have some experiences that were not centered on my grief.

Many bereaved who care for a small, manageable pet are greatly benefited as well. Whether animal or person, nurturing someone else can be a decisive boon.

Bringing Gifts

THE GREATEST GIFT, of course, is your presence. But friends instinctively look for something else to bring...something to fill the emptiness, or at least soften it for a few moments. Yet many people find it difficult to decide what is appropriate to bring.

A book should be carefully chosen and, ideally, short. Books of inspiring quotations, or a story of healing and hope with two-or-three-page chapters, are helpful. The reality of grief is that normal powers of concentration are greatly diminished or absent altogether. Even avid readers find the period of immediate grief to be a time when the usual comfort brought by reading is lost because of inner distractions.

A tape of soothing music which requires no concentration can be immensely helpful. My friend Mary created a CD filled with songs that spoke to her as she grieved the loss of her son. Many of the melodies elicited tears...but the tears were cleansing, and they helped to unlock the great swells of emotion she was feeling within.

I was very moved by some lovely personal gifts — a bottle of perfume, a pretty nightie, a bracelet, a new sweater. I was definitely not concerned with my appearance. Yet the feminine gifts told me that even though I didn't feel beautiful, beauty was neverthe-less still part of life. My femininity had not died with my spouse. That outward sign of beauty was a link to something I'd once known, and would one day em-brace again. Soaps, body lotion, sachets... they all conveyed the same meaning. And since touch is al-ways healing, a gift certificate for a massage is also a wonderful gift to offer.

Flowers are important for both their beauty and their fragrance. They fill the very air. Immediately follow-ing a funeral there are always several bouquets, so consider waiting to send flowers. Estimate when the funeral bouquets will wither, wait a few days more, and then send flowers. The unexpected continuation of love and support helps to ease the hard first days after all the rituals have ended.

Six months later, or on a particular anniversary or holiday, it's helpful to send flowers again. By then the larger support system has naturally diminished, but grief may have intensified. A gift at that time says that you still remember and that the flow of love continues.

Office mates of my friends Allan and Lois gave them a magnolia tree to plant in their garden in memory of their infant daughter, Emily. For years this thoughtful gift will speak of the love of friends and the beauty of Emily's memory.

Even a single rose, especially on a holiday like Valentine's Day, helped me to still feel included in the celebrations enjoyed by everyone else. A friend's flower could not replace the flowers I might have received from my husband. But I was still remembered by someone, and it helped a great deal to ease the pain of that day.

You might give your friend a journal if he or she has any inclination to sort through feelings by writing them down. Keeping a personal journal is also a way to record facts that will fade in memory in spite of your strongest conviction that you will never forget. A written story can become an important record of progress. It is proof of growth in the grieving, as well as an effective way to get in touch with feelings. Once something has been written down and then reread, its clarity is twice as sharp.

I often went for days without writing in my own journal. One entry contained only four words, *I hate my life*. But that page was accurate, recorded history for that day. When I began to reach out to life again, I could see how I had slowly made progress from that time of despair.

A journal is therapeutic because it is a private, confidential place to record strong, honest feelings (like anger) without incurring anyone else's judgment or response. A journal is a safe place to fantasize or yearn. Eventually, when bereaved persons write positively as well as negatively about their lives, the written words reinforce the power of the positive thoughts. As entries are reread, the positive insights help to build a new hope.

The Gift of Time

YOUR TIME is an invaluable gift. Time to help with chores, meals, or caring for children. Time to take a long walk. Time to go to the theater. Time to be together on the anniversary of a birthday or wedding. Time to help fill a long Sunday afternoon or a weekend evening. Time to be a babysitter, relieving parents who are exhausted or perhaps freeing them to attend an important function. Time to help address thank-you notes, to help with correspondence. Time to help a single parent make decisions when another adult's perspective is badly needed. Time to take a fishing or camping trip with older children who've lost a parent. Time to help young children pick out Mother's Day or Father's Day cards or gifts for a single parent.

Offer Your Know-How

THE ORGANIZATIONAL SKILLS or know-how that you may have are also wonderful gifts to offer. For example, your understanding of insurance forms, probate procedures, or taxes can be priceless. You might be able to help with gardening, shoveling snow, or giving handyman advice.

My friend Kit mowed his neighbors' lawn when they were out of town to attend a family funeral. When they returned, tired and beaten, the yard wasn't overgrown, as they'd anticipated. What a boost for a weary morale.

These are the nitty-gritty needs of existence, and while they may seem small, they can be overwhelming when faced alone. I lovingly remember the friends who called me during snowstorms and hurricanes, realizing that facing storms alone might be frightening. These calls were the simplest and smallest gestures, like the plate of cookies I once received on the anniversary of my child's birthday. But I have never forgotten any of them.

Suggest Activities

BE A SUPPORT when the bereaved is ready to take some steps back into the mainstream of life by suggesting projects, involvements, volunteer work, and so on. New beginnings start with small steps, and they are all hard. So include yourself in some of the suggestions for moving forward. *Let's take a course together at the junior college next summer.* Or, as my friend Myrtle suggested, *Let's purchase some season tickets together for Hartford Stage.*

If your friend goes to church, you might offer to accompany him or her. The strong emotions that can rise quickly to the surface in a religious setting sometimes make it difficult to attend religious services. Going with someone else can help immeasurably, especially if the friend is sensitive enough to understand that the bereaved might prefer sitting near the back so he can leave quickly, or possibly a bit early. It may also be helpful to attend a new church for a while, where strangers do not know you and memories are not as sharp.

The Gift of Touch

GIVE THE GIFT of touch. A hand on someone's shoulder, a hug . . . no one knows the importance of touch more than those who live alone and those who grieve. Human touch is an essential transfer of energy. A wordless way of saying, *You're not alone.* Touch interrupts the isolation of grief and momentarily fills the emptiness. In reaching out, you transfer strength and hope. As my friend Susan remembers about the night when her son was killed, "The touch diffused my pain."

The Holidays

IT'S IMPOSSIBLE to predict *which* holidays will be the most painful to celebrate following a loss. Yet it is generally true that the first one or two celebrations of each holiday without the deceased (or following any major loss) are extremely challenging. When death has occurred *on* a holiday, or in close proximity to one, the day is even more complex, and it may never again be experienced without a certain mixture of both joy and pain.

Eleanor, a bereaved parent, described it this way:

I push my shopping cart through Zayre, Kmart, wherever; sometimes I'm not sure which store I'm in. Oh, there's the yarn — I'll get green, red, and white. I toss them all into my cart on top of a Thanksgiving Day card for my uncle, or did I send him one already? Oh, well, it will go to someone, some Thanksgiving.

This was a good day for me, I finally found a pair of jeans that fit me since I've gained the pounds from nervous eating. I stop, watching the activity around me. Decorations are all over; there are none at home. People are buying presents, and the kids finger the packages of candies and stare longingly at stacks of toys and games. No one even notices me, that I seem to stare blankly and wander listlessly, feigning an interest in material texture. "May I help you?" asks the clerk, "No, I'm just looking."

I feel there is a neon sign on my head flashing, "Bereaved parent: handle with care," but no one sees it. Business as usual. They don't know I ate out of desperation because I could not cure my son. Nothing could save him. They don't know that I crochet yarn fast so I can keep my hands busy so my mind doesn't think. I can create something out of yarn, and my child loved my creativity; but nobody here knows my son is dead.

Where do I send my creations? Nobody notices tear-filled eyes as I look at cards that read "Merry Christmas, Mom" — that card won't ever come anymore. Would store security be called if I began to sob and cry out loudly, "Stop the world please, if only for a minute, in respect for my son. He is dead." But I look like an ordinary person.

With poignancy this bereaved mother depicts her breaking heart in the context of a culture that is enjoying and rejoicing. At such times, feelings of disconnection and a sense of standing apart from life's mainstream are great. On other, ordinary, days the divide doesn't seem so wide. On holidays, the distance between your own heartache and the seeming brightness of everything around you is great and stark. The world is celebrating and you are weeping.

As the bereaved anticipates the first holiday, he or she wonders, "How will I behave? What will it be like? What adjustments must I make?" It is common to dread the day and wish it away. The struggle to cope with yet another reminder of all that has changed is an added burden. It hurts to be in pain when the world is joyful; it hurts to realize that your loved one will never be there to celebrate holidays again. Many things will eventually fall into place, but some things will never be the same.

Encourage your friend to mark the holiday in ways that are best for her. It isn't a matter of avoiding pain; that will be impossible. It's a matter of *managing* pain in the best way possible. Allow your friend to be honest about what to expect and what they are able to do.

If necessary, support the bereaved in a need to alter their usual celebration. These are the moments when "the way we've always done things" may be changed. Tradition comforts some hearts, and it breaks others. Let the bereaved know that it's okay not to function as usual. It's okay for her to take care of herself, and not exhaust herself doing what is comfortable for everyone else. It's okay to make changes. Change the seating around the table. Serve different dishes. Have the meal at a different time. Many grieving persons find a local soup kitchen and serve meals there. What matters is creating a plan that will best get everyone through these very difficult times. New arrangements are not forever binding. The bereaved can always return to traditional ways of celebrating in future years. The only decision that needs to be made is for today.

Ways You Can Help

REGARDLESS OF whether or not the manner of celebrating a holiday changes, the holidays will be different for those who grieve. Encourage the bereaved not to overextend, to plan a holiday strategy well in advance, having the courage to do what truly helps them the most. Planning ahead is the key. Encourage them to acknowledge and accept any feelings that arise, and not to set unreasonable expectations for themselves, like feeling joyful or even the same as they used to feel.

As a friend, you might offer to help the bereaved with holiday shopping. Many bereaved parents find it extremely difficult to enter toy stores to purchase gifts for other children on their list. Sometimes just facing holiday decorations and hearing holiday music is difficult. You might accompany your friend on such shopping trips, perhaps driving to stores that are less familiar and where fewer memories will be triggered. Or, if you can, help the bereaved to shop through catalogs or by using the Internet. You might even run errands for them.

The third Christmas following my loss, and after I'd bought a house, a church member named Charlie Lewis cut down a tree from his tree farm, delivered it, and put it up for me. There will never be a Christmas when I don't remember Charlie and his wonderful way of helping me make it through those first holidays.

It can be surprising when the painful times also include some unexpected moments of fun. Enjoying life again is not a betrayal of the person who died, even if it feels that way. Levity and happiness are life-giving for overextended systems, and they are a great tribute to someone you loved. They affirm that your relationship will live on not only in tears, but also in joy.

Specific Holidays

New Year's Day is difficult for many because it signifies new beginnings. For those longing for the past, looking ahead only accentuates their loss. The reality that life goes on is not comforting when you ache to make time stand still. Other people are partying, and you are facing life alone. Three hundred and sixty-five days — empty, unwanted days — stretch ahead of you.

It might help to encourage your grieving friend to be with you for a portion of the evening. Also encourage him or her to break the year ahead into smaller pieces. Instead of thinking *how will I make it through the next year?*, consider only getting through January. Take one month at a time. Even one week, one day at a time. Be creative and give your friend a calendar that you have torn apart, but deliver it month by month.

Valentine's Day, or any day especially dedicated to couples and to love, is painful for those who have been part of a couple and are suddenly alone. They may feel distanced from the mainstream of life and cheated out of some of life's richness. Any small remembrance on that day will help them feel included, especially if you communicate that you remember the lost loved one as well. Your flowers or chocolates won't be the remembrance for which your friend's heart longs, but they will still matter. My own piano used to be lined with Valentine cards from caring friends. Each card and remembrance became a visible string of love.

Mother's Day and Father's Day are particularly difficult when a child or parent has died. It is also important to remember that a widow or widower with young children has lost the spouse who initiated the remembrances of that day. Men who have lost children often feel an especially poignant grief on Father's Day since our culture ties men's identities and masculinity to their success in providing for and protecting women and children.

Help the bereaved on these days by sending a simple card or note of remembrance. Take them to dinner. Couples are still mothers and fathers, whether or not their children are alive. Help younger children purchase a card or create a gift for their single parent. And support parents in ignoring the day entirely, if that's what they need to do. Whatever is planned, it usually helps to keep it simple.

After losing her only child in early May, Theresa remembered, "I was so angry not to be remembered on Mother's Day, except by my brother, who bought me a pocketbook. I cried all day. I just didn't know what to do with myself."

Thanksgiving, Christmas, Hanukkah, Rosh Hashanah, and Ramadan are times for family and family celebration. They arouse feelings of anticipation, along with a subtle sense that maybe our longings for happiness really *can* be fulfilled. For those who grieve, the great disparity between the pain in their hearts and the culture's outer celebrations can hurt deeply. Changing the usual rituals is helpful for many. But expect that there will still be pain.

Another approach is to *add* new traditions that acknowledge the loss. But keep in mind that familiar traditions may be very important for children. Mary wrote, "Retaining many of our holiday traditions gave our surviving children an important sense of stability in the wake of profound loss and unwelcome changes. Some of their requests were painful to honor, but my husband and I felt they were crucial for our children's healing."

The Effect of Grief on Families

EVERY SURVIVING family member shares the grief when a child or parent dies. Typically, in the loss of a parent, both the spouse and children receive attention fairly evenly. However, in the loss of a child, the grief of surviving siblings often receives much less focus than the loss of the grieving parents.

Death of a sibling is a confusing and tumultuous time for surviving brothers and sisters. In some sense they initially lose their parents as well, because the parents who normally guide them through crises are in need of comfort themselves. The family system is hurting, as well as the individuals.

Bereaved siblings, like their parents, experience anger, guilt, fright, and loneliness. In addition, the loss is likely to be their first major occasion to face life's unfairness. Powerful emotions may rage within, and they may be poorly equipped to acknowledge or release these feelings.

It is common for children to feel like failures because they can't make their parents feel better, or because grief over a brother or sister seems to indicate that the living child's presence is no comfort or has little meaning.

Friends or other relatives can be invaluable when they step in and supplement the limited attention from shattered parents. If the family is willing, you might arrange to take siblings out of the home for a change of scenery or an afternoon's activity. Always provide time to listen. Let children know that talking about their sister or brother is welcomed. Hug them, and let them feel loved. Remember them on special occasions that may not be celebrated as usual at home. Help them celebrate holidays their parents may be unable to face. In a sense, the surrounding adults can become a vital extended family.

Children sometimes act as if the death has not occurred. Integrating the loss will take time. They may also complain of physical symptoms and be afraid that they, too, will die.

Younger children grieve very sporadically. Following a burst of tears, they run out to play. They seem to possess an innate sense that "growing up" cannot be put on hold. A child who plays baseball following his mother's death is not uncaring. This is simply a child's way. A child's grief is very likely to be expressed indirectly. For instance, he or she may suddenly burst into tears following the scrape of a knee, or another child's teasing, in disproportion to the actual circumstance.

It is natural for children to wonder who will take care of them, or even to think that their anger with a sibling or parent "caused" their death. *If I'd been better, they wouldn't have died.* It is a tumultuous time. Sometimes children regress, reverting to behaviors they have long ago outgrown. It is all part of the grief cycle. However, if they have not begun to resume normal behavior in six months or so, it's wise to speak with teachers, a pediatrician, or a professional counselor for advice.

Do allow children to be part of family discussions about the parent or child who died. It is reassuring to children to know that others are deeply saddened too, but they will still be taken care of. Children need to hear that there is enough love to go around. If they are never part of conversations about the deceased, they may imagine a much scarier story than any tearful conversation might reveal. Remember that each child, like each adult, copes with grief in a unique way. Listen to them and answer their questions with care.

Teenagers also struggle to fully express their grief and feelings of anger and confusion. It is not unusual for their immediate grief to be very muted. Then, typically in the twenties, the grief they were emotionally and psychologically unprepared to face when they were young suddenly confronts them. Often another death or the hurtful ending of a relationship will trigger their emotions. At any age, it helps to be around friends who create openings for grief and express a willingness to have conversation. But the readiness to actually address the pain has its own individual timetable.

Practical Ideas

LOIS AND ALLAN'S family remembers their daughter, Emily, with an annual family tradition. Each member makes a Christmas tree ornament for Emily, symbolizing his or her own relationship to the loss. Some families create journals or pieces of art that give voice to their memories. Others create photo albums, memory quilts, or wall hangings. Each creation reaches into the family system, encouraging healing.

My friend Betty lost her daughter, Megan, in 1974. Each year at Thanksgiving, Betty and her family pack a food basket for a needy family, and they do so in Megan's memory. The basket not only helps another family, but it gives the love Betty's family has for Megan a new road to travel.

Some families create a sanctuary for grief within the home. Mary wrote, "Our family dedicated an alcove in our study for this purpose. We retreated there when we felt the need to honor our grief, or when our grief became overwhelming. If it wasn't possible to go there as often as we needed, the car sometimes became a sanctuary of sorts for my husband and me. It was a place where we could listen to moving music or inspirational tapes and have a really good cry in total privacy.

"We also reminded ourselves that despite our tragedy, we were still incredibly blessed. The more we chose to focus on the present, living 'in the now,' the less painful our existence was. There were days when this was very difficult to do, but the effort always paid off. We even found a journal called *Gratitude: A Record of Your Blessing*. It's a beautiful reminder."

Something to think about...

What can you do for your grieving friend during the next holiday?

The Pattern of Grief

PROGRESS THROUGH GRIEF is difficult to judge by outward appearances. One good day may be followed by two weeks of wrenching tears and anger — anger that the bereaved (and probably others) assumed was in the past. These patterns of back-and-forth, advance and retreat, are part of the complex nature of grief. Grief is not linear. You don't feel steadily better day by day. You feel better, and then you feel worse — over and over again. However, the ground that is won on a good day is never lost. Every small victory is indelible. Grief is a process of small victories building upon each other until a day when the victories dominate.

For some reason, especially in the loss of a child, pain is most often pronounced five to six months following a loss. By then the greatest shock has begun to wear off, and the impact of life without the one who is gone seems to settle in with new intensity. At the same time, attentions that surrounded the newly bereaved are diminishing. Life is now seen as it is and as it will be. *This is really my life.* The vision can be grim. Each of these factors creates a period of new despair.

At this crossing my friend Theresa wrote in her journal, "I can go on without him. How dare I? But I can. I feel like a betrayer." Such realizations tear the heart. This is why, after seeming to "do so well" for many weeks, the bereaved may suddenly seem to be slipping, as if they'd been struck a second time. This isn't a step backward, although it feels that way. This period is really a tear-filled step forward, ironically made possible *because* of the grieving previously experienced and because of the steps already taken. The layers of grief peel back in turn, but only after certain plateaus have been reached. Going to the next deepest level is a sure sign that work at the preceding level was accomplished. A friend's understanding of this rhythm of grief can offer much-needed support in these times.

The first year, though difficult, is usually somewhat softened by the presence of shock. The bereaved may still be numb until the second year, when stark reality is felt more deeply and a greater suffering is experienced. Don't assume that once the bereaved has made it through the first year she is past the worst. Equal (even greater) compassion may be needed in the year that follows. Don't stop reaching out too soon.

My friend Lois wrote, "Don't be hurt if I can't share in your joy (wedding, new baby, child's milestone) in my usual way. Any ceremonial occasion can make my pain sharper.

"Don't be surprised if another, smaller loss makes me react out of proportion to the cause (for example, a pet's death following the loss of a spouse) — the new hurt can summon up all the pain of the first major loss.

"Please understand if I'm oversensitive, touchy, or prone to misinterpreting your words or gestures.

"Please be patient if it takes me an extra-long time to finish a task. I am doing the best I can."

Reassure the bereaved that she is not falling apart or permanently regressing and that you are still there for her. She needs to hear that this is simply another phase of the grief journey. In fact, it is a vital phase. Until the pain of grief is faced squarely, full healing will not take place, and lasting progress cannot be made. Those who grieve and reach new plateaus momentarily cry harder tears *because* of the strength of the grief work they have already done. New tears may move them inward again for a while, but eventually they will continue moving forward.

Limit Major Decisions

GRIEF IS PERSONAL, and people are unique. One person's solution may be another person's disaster. There are no generic timetables for the many decisions that grief raises (for example, when to remove a wedding band, when to put away clothes, or when to change a room). There is, nevertheless, one wisdom that applies to everyone: *Whenever possible, limit major decisions or changes for a year after a loss. Wait for a full set of four seasons to pass.*

Even those who believe themselves to be functioning well during the first year of grief are still not
functioning with complete clarity. A desire to diminish pain is active in the best of us, and this desire can
skew judgment. It is a rare individual who makes the
same caliber of choice during this time that she might
make when not feeling so intensely lonely, frightened,
or filled with pain.

The first year is a time of intense change, and because of that, it is a time to settle, wait, and sort . . . not
to forge ahead. This is especially true in the aftermath
of sudden, accidental deaths. Friends and family who
are informed can protect the bereaved by encouraging them to wait one year before making changes that
may have important or long-lasting effects.

During my first year of grief, in fact in the first weeks,
I allowed myself to plunge into decisions where the
proverbial angels would fear to tread. My simultaneous
loss of husband and child already merited me a high-
risk score on any psychological stress chart. Added to
that were the realities of pregnancy, my own injuries
from the accident, the emotional impact of *being* in
the accident, and a sudden, major change in financial
status. Added to *that* was shock. Even so, I plunged
ahead and made major decisions.

In a one-month period immediately following my
losses, I moved from my residence, away from all
of my friends. In fact, I moved to another state. This
meant packing all my belongings, half of which I gave

away on the spot. I gave away treasured items as well as expensive and useful household equipment. I believed, in that moment, that I would never again live in a house, never need a lawn mower or ladder. . . . I gave away a wooden chest that my husband had made for me when we were engaged. On the top of the chest he had carved words especially for me. I sold it without blinking. I just wanted the pain to go away, and in that moment, I thought that if I couldn't physically see the reminders, the pain would diminish.

Within three months I regretted moving so quickly from my familiar surroundings, and I was appalled at what I had given away. At great expense and with considerable emotional strain, I began to pack for a second time to move back to my former town. For three months I'd struggled with pharmacies that were unfamiliar, strange doctors, and acquiring a new driver's license, registration, and insurance. It was too much. Too much change, too much newness. I felt as if I would go mad inside if at least some of my outer surroundings didn't reflect what I already knew. My family system was different; my insides felt like a foreign land. I needed at least some outer markers that were stable.

Because of my initial hasty move, I was now minus many things that I had treasured or needed. In some cases I didn't even remember giving the items away.

The wisdom in waiting a year is to give the bereaved person the greatest opportunity to get back to both an inner and an outer equilibrium. It's a time to proceed slowly. Pain tempts the bereaved person to believe that changing homes or locations will reduce the pain. The truth is that the turmoil and pain the bereaved feels is *in them*, and it will go with them wherever they go. There is no foolproof place to flee to. You will face the grief work in a new location, or in familiar surroundings. Grief can't be cheated. No place feels "right" until *you* are right. It usually helps to grieve in a familiar place. The "loss" of familiar surroundings can become an additional grief.

In the immediate hours surrounding grief, hasty decisions are often made. At that time, when the pain is most acute, many acts seem as if they will excise the hurt. But of course they do not.

Theresa wrote, "When Ronny [her nearly two-year-old son] first went into the hospital for his cancerous tumor, I longed to get back to his room and touch his toys. I longed to remember how his bed and clothes smelled prior to his illness.

"But when we knew his death was imminent, and before we returned from our long hospital stay, I asked my mom if she would go to his room and remove everything. Suddenly I couldn't tolerate the thought of any reminders.

"She did a thorough job. She changed beds and washed clothes, even vacuumed Ronny's footprints from the carpet. When we came home there was nothing left of the Ronny we knew. I made such a mistake."

Continuing Support

GRIEF EXPERTS agree that a person is grieving "well" when she eventually faces her grief in some way. Perhaps by talking. Crying. Writing. By releasing anger verbally, or through physical exercise. In whatever way grief is expressed, the period of initial shock should begin to fade and improvements in daily functioning should be visible by the second year. For some, those improvements are small and barely perceptible; for others, large strides will have been taken. Since grief is unique to each individual, expect tremendous fluctuations in the improvements experienced by different persons in the second year. But some degree of advance should be seen. Perhaps the moments of respite between the waves of pain will have lengthened. But if pain experienced in the second year is as all-encompassing as it was in the first year (with no efforts made to return to normal functioning), then help should be sought.

For most people the fleeting "good periods," when life is still experienced with some savor, should lengthen. By the second year, some persons make considerable adjustments. They may plan to remarry, or they may be ready to give birth to (or adopt) another child. It is the norm for some, not for others.

For those whose outward progress is slower, facing the inner loss may only now be at its peak. The cushion of shock is gone, and the periods of pain, when they arrive, are felt more deeply. Many people wake up one morning in the second year with the realization, *This is really my life. This is it.* These raw realizations cause the second year to be emotionally crushing. Pain, without shock, is now felt to its deepest extent.

This new, sharper pain feels incredibly defeating, and it's easy to conclude, *If after a year the pain is even deeper, then I'll never get better.* But the deeper pain and the stark reality actually herald progress. Pain must be faced; healing demands it. So whenever pain is confronted, the healing process is gaining.

As a friend, don't withdraw your support after the first year. Even though the bereaved may have resumed her day-to-day functions, the inner awareness of loss may never be greater. Make allowance for this, and continue to create opportunities to talk. Also stretch your understanding, and allow for bleak moods and newly dampened spirits. The bereaved may need you in the second year as much as in the beginning stages of grieving.

Mary offered, "At the end of every year I pen a letter to our friends that details our grief journey and the lessons we've learned along the way. This has been cathartic for me, and many people have mentioned that the letters have helped them with their personal hardships and consequent faith struggles."

A widow or widower sometimes finds himself or herself "uninvited" to join the same circle of couples they were part of before the death of a spouse. Everyone initially supported them in their loss, but when friends resumed their social patterns and the normal rhythms of their lives, the invitations gradually dwindled. This is less typical for senior citizens, but it's very typical when the widowed person is young, especially for women. The sudden absence of invitations is hurtful. It suggests that you have not only lost a spouse, but also your social life. In strong terms it tells the widowed person that because she is alone, she no longer fits in. Society is geared for couples.

With a little sensitivity and forethought, a widowed person can be successfully included at gatherings of couples. The most awkward moments usually surround issues like transportation and paying the bill in a restaurant. When I was asked and given an opportunity to state my preference honestly beforehand, I was always more comfortable. I might say, *I'd like to ride with you so I won't have to drive alone,* or *I'd like to give you some money beforehand so you can handle my bill at the restaurant.* It did *not* feel comfortable to be treated like an invalid or to always be "treated" to the movie or meal. Widowhood made me feel enough like a fifth wheel without letting my inclusion in a social evening cause even more special treatment.

The sharpest hurt for widowed persons can occur when friends surprise them with a date — the eligible man or woman who "just happens" to arrive as a dinner partner or theater companion. Such surprises can feel very demeaning, even if you, as a friend, had good intentions. It suggests that everyone else is awkward if the bereaved is not partnered, or that their presence alone is not enough. Or perhaps that only being part of a twosome is acceptable. The friend who arranges such a surprise never intends it to backfire, but it may.

You can help the most by being candid. Simply ask what your friend prefers. Even if he or she declines an invitation (weddings and New Year's Eve parties are particularly difficult), it still matters that you asked. An invitation is a strong message that your friend is not forgotten.

After being widowed for a decade, I never felt completely comfortable joining couples for an evening when I was the only single person present. But being asked to join friends *did* matter. And sitting at home because I'd refused an invitation was a world apart from knowing that everyone was getting together and I hadn't been included.

Creative Invitations

INVITATIONS THAT WERE both candid and creative were the most helpful for me. Some couples asked if I'd like to see them separately, as individuals, rather than as couples; others asked if meeting in a public place without the vivid reminders of anyone's home would be easier.

When parents lose an only child, it can be awkward to reenter their old social world. They no longer relate as a family getting together with other families. They will no longer be participating in the activities that were child-centered. Even parents who are suddenly "single" have to adjust and ask themselves, *How will I fit in as a single parent?*

Friends help tremendously by issuing invitations to include those who grieve, especially during the holidays. If you do invite someone who is grieving, it's an extra courtesy to tell your guest who will be there and what the day (or evening) will be like. Knowing that, I could always judge whether or not I'd feel comfortable at their celebration. When the invitation was also issued with the spoken understanding that I could accept or refuse until the last moment, or leave as soon as I needed to, I appreciated it doubly.

Over the years several families in Connecticut invited my daughter Beth and me to join them for various holidays. They were careful to describe what their traditions and schedules were like. There was never any pressure on me to accept the invitation, and there was no sense of hurt if I refused. The times when Beth and I joined these families created rich memories, and I'm certain they will never know what those times meant to us. Even when I refused, staying at home knowing there had been an invitation was totally different from staying at home because there was no place to go.

Our friends Laura and Chuck further proved how creative and reaching love could be. When I was first widowed and had newly given birth, they had not yet begun their own family. Christmas morning was painful for me, yet it was also terribly important to me to create good Christmas morning memories for Beth. So Laura and Chuck offered to come to our home to help. For years I phoned them on Christmas morning as soon as Beth was awake, at whatever hour, and they would arrive within minutes. Their presence helped me through the early years in a way I could never express. After opening gifts and sharing a fancy breakfast, they returned to their own home, and I could have the quiet I needed. The hardest hours were now behind me.

Something to think about...

As your friend works through her grief, especially in the first two years, in what creative ways can you be a support?

Other Infant Losses

 EVERY GRIEF has one thing in common: those who grieve desperately need the understanding and sensitivity of good friends. This is especially true in the loss of an infant.

Those who lose a child through miscarriage, stillbirth, or a newborn death often feel that others dismiss their loss. *Since you didn't really know this child, how deep can the grief be?* The loss isn't treated as a "real" loss, or it is treated as something that is easily resolved. *Don't worry, you'll have another child.*

The truth is that expectant parents deeply anticipate *any* birth. They have invested hope and love in the child's safe arrival. They have created a dream for their future. When the child dies, not only is the dream never realized, but it is also taken away without any experience of fulfillment, of meeting their child. There are no comforting memories. A grieving mother is especially susceptible to the question, *What did I do wrong?* She may be sorely tempted to consider herself unfit biologically and to feel that she has failed.

Friends help the most by understanding and honoring the significant loss. The couple has lost a child. They hurt. And although attention flows primarily to the mother who has physically borne the infant, the loss is different, but of no less significance, for the expectant father. His dreams died too. Both parents

123

have feelings of helplessness and disappointment. In addition, when death is the result of a miscarriage, throughout the following months they will know at what stage they "would have been" in their pregnancy. When full-term birth would have occurred, reach out to them. This can be a particularly painful time.

Unmentionable Deaths

SURVIVAL OF EVERY LOSS is wounding. Yet there is a special hurt experienced by those whose loved ones died by an act of suicide or by any other so-called "unmentionable" death, such as drug-related, alcohol-related, or AIDS-related deaths. Survivors of these deaths may be heavily burdened by a sense of failure and responsibility as well as by a loss of self-esteem. Their hearts ache with the questions, *What did I do wrong? How did I fail? What didn't I notice? How might I have done things differently?* Added to the drama and grief is a deep sense of shame for the way death occurred. And added to that is anger. Following her father's suicide, my friend Cheryl wrote, "Why in a dream (nightmare) did you shoot me in the back? Because that's how I feel. . . . This is why suicide hurts: someone didn't give us another chance . . . to care, to understand, to help, to. . . . Others don't really understand the ugly side of survival...pain, anger, fear that mingles with compassion, love, freedom. Suicide is the ultimate rejection."

Friends help by not pulling back. Don't be afraid to approach the bereaved, willing to listen. For these survivors, death has dealt a double blow: loss of a loved one and loss of their own self-confidence and respect. They easily assume that others are judging them as parents or spouses: *Why didn't you know? Why didn't you see the signs?* As a friend, affirm their gifts and their strengths.

My friends Jim and Priscilla survived the suicide of their daughter. They grieved as all parents grieve, but with an added sense of shame and lowered confidence. Then, in conversation, the priest in their parish suggested that they would be excellent candidates to be foster parents. Priscilla recalls that his affirmation was not only pleasing, but also healing. It said that they still had value and worth as people and as parents. Their daughter's act did not devalue their gifts or their ability to love and nurture a child. One person's belief in them planted an important seed.

There are countless creative ways to affirm those who grieve an "unmentionable" death. Solicit their advice. Nominate them for positions of responsibility and trust. Ask them to teach or care for other youth. Persist in affirming them. The healing power of love is greater than shame.

A Grief Calendar

❧ AS TIME GOES ON, consider keeping an informal calendar of the important dates surrounding someone's loss. Jot down the date and year of the death, also marking birthdays, anniversaries, and the period six months and one year following the loss. When the special days arrive, the calendar will remind you to pay a visit, write a card, call, send flowers, and so on. Two or three words of remembrance are a tangible form of love.

Planting Seeds of Strength and Hope

❧ ABOUT A YEAR after my losses I had a brief meeting and conversation with Dr. Norman Vincent Peale, the beloved and internationally respected minister. I remember how fragile I felt as I walked into his office. Terrified, really. *What would he say to me?*

Dr. Peale asked me to tell him my story, and he listened with great love. I was broken and wounded, still reeling with pain. "Paula, I believe you will overcome this," he said to me. Six words. *I believe you will overcome this*. It didn't seem possible at that moment, but I wished the words to be true. With all my heart, I wished them to be true. And their powerful effect was to plant a seed of hope and belief within me.

In succeeding years I have sat with hundreds of other grieving parents or widows who, like me, thought they would never recover from the blow of death. I've looked into many defeated eyes. And in my own way I've tried to pass on the great gift that Dr. Peale gave to me. I've told these survivors that pain does not have the final say. If they choose to, they *can* heal.

As a friend to one who grieves, you cannot choose healing for someone. But you can plant seeds with your words that will give the bereaved person every advantage. Remind those who grieve of their strength and of the power that lies within them. Remind them that there is healing equal to all pain. The end is not sadness. The final say is love. The bereaved desperately need assurances that their intense pain will not last forever.

Making Choices about Healing

DEATH CHANGES hopes and dreams. It thwarts the most careful plans and robs survivors of their innocence. Whether it is accepted graciously or with kicking and screaming, when someone grieves, he or she is changed. Following the changes wrought by grief are the decisions it imposes.

Going on is a choice. The circumstances that brought loss can never be altered. But what we do next — how we decide to live the rest of our lives — is up to us. Healing is not a chance of fate. It is a choice. And sometimes it takes a courageous friend to help the bereaved face that truth.

Allan and Lois, as grieving parents, received this letter from a close friend, Cubby:

> You have been in my thought constantly. There are so many things in my life which I have been able to square away neatly — complete with how and why — but Emily's death is not one of them. . . .
>
> I would guess that your pain comes from being suddenly left with an overwhelming volume of love — and no one to give it to. Sort of like those full breasts of yours, Lois, and all that milk. The milk will go to waste. The love will not. . . . I would guess that the best way to dissipate the love would be to break it up into small pieces and give it away. . . . You will give it away piece by piece, and every time you do you will say quietly, "Here. This is from Emily and me."

In the face of loss, it's never that we can't love again or be happy again. It's that we either will or we won't.

Nearly three years after my losses, I was still living in the past, handcuffed to memories of what I had lost. I'd made sizable outer adjustments, but in my heart I was still tied to yesterday. Then my friend Paul confronted me. "You see yourself only as a grieving widow and mother," he said. "Nothing more. You're not choosing to live your life today. You've given up on the person you were meant to be."

His words stung and angered me. How dare he? I didn't want to be challenged; I wanted sympathy. I wanted comfort. It was a while before I could see that his words were not filled with judgment; they were motivated by love. When I finally heard the plea in Paul's words, I saw them as a challenge to live as if I were alive. Madeleine L'Engle taught me, "Grief doesn't leave you. *You* leave grief." In my heart of hearts I didn't want to live half-asleep, clinging to grief. I didn't want the final tribute of my life to be the fact that knowing Roy and Sarah had diminished love in me. What could be more senseless? Because of knowing them, I wanted love to *increase* in me. So I took up Paul's challenge and set in motion the final stage of my healing. I decided to fully live.

Epilogue

GRIEF HAS BEEN both my great teacher and the hardest work I have ever done. It cut me in two, excising my innocence and my illusions. When the scar began to mend, new awarenesses began to replace the illusions. I learned that everyday choices are powerful. Through them, life is either grasped or deflected. I became willing to learn from everything. I began asking, *What is life trying to tell me through this experience?* I became more honest. I observed a world where there is more emphasis on being perfect than being real. I chose to be real. I discovered that victorious people have primarily overcome self, not circumstances.

I learned to be gentle with myself, and I learned that there is no right way. My deepest grief was private. And sometimes the deep sadness I was feeling was not the immediate loss, but other losses that surfaced in its wake. Some losses lie buried until the searchlight of grief illuminates them. Anything I'd failed to address came up for review. I bore with it. Steven Levine wrote, "Acute grief is a thunderstorm, a monsoonal downpour, a sudden flood that submerges almost everything in its path." Each layer of grief pried at my heart. Grief pried and pried until my heart reopened. I think that was its intention all along.

I learned that love is a single force, and that even though we may lose an expression of love in a particular, tangible form, we never lose love. I learned that my relationship with those who have died is not severed by death. I still know them, but no longer by their wonderful physical presence. I know them in spirit, within my heart, in a new way. And it all took time.

At first, I felt connected to my loved ones only through the pain of loss. But that gradually changed. I learned to connect with them through the love we'd shared. It was a different experience that took me out of the past and into my heart.

In the beginning I despaired of ever drawing a pain-free breath. But one day I looked around and could recognize beauty, hope, and the fleeting preciousness of things. When Roy and Sarah lost their lives, I'd never known such silence. I crawled into the silence and let it take me over. I've probably never listened so deeply, with so much cause not to. Surveying my life, I can't think of what has hurt more or been the means for more gain. Ultimately, the very grief that wounded me made me rich with sight. And sometimes, now, I weep because of how much is possible, how we might live.

I welcome the storm as my terrible guest
It thunders through my bones, washing shadows
from my soul
and leaves . . . my heart cleansed
my wings new
my fears at rest.

—© Alison Asher

Notes

Page 9 / Alison Asher, *Soaring into the Storm* (Seattle: Life Skills Press, 1996), 27.

Page 12 / Jim Wallis, "Micah, Bono and the Chancellor of the Exchequer," speech given at the Los Angeles Religious Education Congress, Anaheim, CA, February 2005.

Page 14 / Asher, *Soaring into the Storm*, 20.

Page 18 / "Argue for your limitations...": Richard Bach, *Illusions* (New York: Delacorte Press, 1977), 75.

Page 23 / "Choosing not to die...": Anne Wilson Schaef, *When Society Becomes an Addict* (HarperSanFrancisco, 1987), 16.

Page 24 / "You cannot see the storms...": Asher, *Soaring into the Storm*, 25.

Page 68 / Asher, *Soaring into the Storm*, 58.

Page 130 / "Acute grief is a thunderstorm...": Stephen Levine, *Unattended Sorrow* (New York: Rodale, 2005), 11.

Page 131 / "I welcome the storm as my terrible guest...": Asher, *Soaring into the Storm*, 37. Reprinted by permission of the poet.

Suggested Reading List

Asher, Alison. *Soaring into the Storm* (Seattle: LifeSkills Press, 1996)

Baumgardner, Barbara, *A Passage through Grief* (Nashville: Broadman and Holman Publishers, 1997).

Bayly, Joe, *The Last Thing We Talk About* (Colorado Springs, CO: David C. Cook, 1969).

Berry, Carmen and Mary Ellen, *Reawakening to Life* (New York: Crossroad Publishing Company, 2002).

Bosco, Antoinette, *The Pummeled Heart* (Mystic, CT: Twenty-Third Publications, 1993).

Brooks, Anne M., *The Grieving Time* (New York: Harmony Books, 1985).

Callanan, Maggie, and Patricia Kelley, *Final Gifts* (New York: Bantam Books, 1993).

Claypool, John, *Tracks of a Fellow Struggler* (Nashville: W Publishing Group, 1974).

D'Arcy, Paula, *Gift of the Red Bird* (New York: Crossroad Publishing Company, 1996).

D'Arcy, Paula, *Song for Sarah* (Colorado Springs, CO: WaterBrook Press, 2001).

Dawson, Ann, *A Season of Grief* (Notre Dame, IN: Ave Maria Press, 2002).

Estes, Clarissa Pinkola, *The Faithful Gardener* (HarperSanFrancisco, 1995).

Fumia, Molly, *Safe Passage* (Boston: Conari Press, 1992).

Gilbert, Richard, *Finding Your Way after Your Parent Dies* (Notre Dame, IN: Ave Maria Press, 1999).

LeShan, Eda, *Learning to Say Good-By: When a Parent Dies* (New York: Avon, 1976).

Levine, Stephen, *Unattended Sorrow* (Emmaus, PA: Rodale, 2005).

Lukas, Christopher, and Henry M. Seiden, Ph.D., *Silent Grief: Living in the Wake of Suicide* (New York: Macmillan Publishing Company, 1987).

Mellonie, Bryan, and Robert Ingpen, *Lifetimes: The Beautiful Way to Explain Death to Children* (New York: Bantam, 1983).

Poole, Charles E., *Is Life Fair?* (Macon, GA: Smyth & Helwys Publishing, 1996).

Rupp, Joyce, *Praying Our Goodbyes* (Notre Dame, IN: Ave Maria Press, 1988).

Rupp, Joyce, *Your Sorrow Is My Sorrow* (New York: Crossroad Publishing Company, 1999).

Shaw, Luci, *God in the Dark* (Grand Rapids, MI: Zondervan, 1989).

Smith, Harold Ivan, *GriefKeeping* (New York: Crossroad Publishing Company, 2004).

Smith, Harold Ivan, and Steven L. Jeffers, *ABC's of Healthy Grieving: Light for a Dark Journey* (Shawnee Mission, KS: Shawnee Mission Medical Center Foundation, 2001).

Acknowledgments

I AM ALWAYS GRATEFUL to the whole Crossroad team, this time especially to Roy M. Carlisle and John Jones, who have encouraged me to revise this work. Any author who finds even one editor who believes in her work has a great treasure. Roy and John are steady sources of support and creativity. It makes a difference. And my gratitude to Shirley Coe for her faultless copyediting.

My daughter Beth is a continuous joy. Because of her, in 1975, I kept going. Now a beautiful young woman, she works as my personal assistant...but more importantly, shares the vision of helping others see what is possible in their lives.

And to family, friends, and fellow grievers, I give my grateful love. No listing of names could be complete. But these are the individuals who contributed directly to the grief journey told in these pages: Beverly Pettine, Barbara Barnes, Sandy Broden, Kaye Bernard, David Smith, Mary Cox, Susan Goldby, Madeline Tyng, Susan Oakley, Kirby Hlavaty, Joyce Rupp, Macrina Wiederkehr, Richard Rohr, Nancy Connery, Anne Kastner, Glenna Butler, Lois Lake Church, Allan Church, Robin Hebert, Easton Hebert, Jim Maxwell, Betsy Maxwell, Cheryl Marchand, Theresa Lipeika. And my grateful thanks to all the others mentioned in this text, or whose words are quoted.

Special thanks to co-star Tony Navarra who tours with me in the performance of my one-act play, *On My Way Home*. Through the performance of my own story of loss, healing, and hope, I have continued to heal, and Tony's portrayal of God has contributed richly to that healing (see *www.redbirdfoundation.com* for itinerary).

About the Author

PAULA D'ARCY, a writer, retreat leader, and conference and seminar speaker, travels widely in the United States, Canada, and abroad. She is president of the Red Bird Foundation, which supports the growth and spiritual development of those in need and furthers a ministry both to those in prison and those living in disadvantaged cultures.

A former psychotherapist who has ministered to Morrie Schwartz and others facing issues of grief and loss, Paula worked with the Peale Foundation, founded by Dr. Norman Vincent Peale, from 1980 until his death in 1993. In recent years, she has teamed with Fr. Richard Rohr in presenting seminars on Male/Female Journey. Her individual work includes leading women in Initiation and Rites of Passage.

Paula's ministry grew from personal tragedy. In 1975 she survived a drunk driving accident which took the lives of her husband and twenty-one-month-old daughter. Pregnant at the time, Paula survived the accident to give birth to a second daughter, Beth Starr.

A Word from the Editor

WHEN I WAS YOUNG I cared most about what I was going to "get to do" in my life, as did all of my friends. Then in middle age I began to wonder what it all meant, since I had experienced a lot more than I had anticipated. Now in my more mature years I care about *how* life's experiences have changed us after we have lived through them. Do we see more, do we see "behind," do we actually hear more, or do we actually seem bigger on the inside than we are on the outside? Usually now I can tell these things very quickly. Authenticity has a ring about it, a certain emotional feel to it that is unmistakable. And the "truth" that I most dislike is that authenticity seems most likely to grow and emerge if we have suffered and embraced our pain. I can't get around it, I can't wish it away, and I can't seem to meet anyone who avoids pain and still seems deeply authentic. Embracing pain is almost like an art form, an emotional art form. And I am not sure how you learn to do it or even who taught me how to do it. But we have to do it, in smaller and bigger ways. Or if we don't do it, as the case may be, then we don't really grow up. For me, the demanding role of religious faith in my life, the agony and ecstasy of raising and relating to my three birth daughters and two honorary daughters, the simple joys but mind-bending demands of my work in book publishing (the anniversary of my twenty-eighth

year as a book editor just slipped by in 2005), my new
forcibly disciplined life as a diabetic, my eclectic but
amazing group of adult friends, and finally my regular encounters with Paula have all helped me embrace
"the difficulty and pain" of life in myriad ways.

When you read a book by Paula D'Arcy you find that
she has embraced pain so deeply that it often startles
you. It also makes you realize that you can embrace
more of it, if you dare. If you want to grow. If you want
to really see, or hear, or live.

It is not always comfortable to be around people who
embrace pain and loss and grief because it reminds us
of our own pain. Of course it is even more uncomfortable to be around those who have not embraced their
pain or loss or grief, because they transmit it through a
certain negative humor, or witty cynicism, or just plain
cruelty. But spending time with those who have embraced the deeper pain of life challenges us to accept
that life is difficult and thereby grow in unanticipated
ways. Ultimately we either decide to accept the challenge of the discomfort we feel around people who are
willing to live authentically with their pain, or we let life
slip by, usually by subtle dynamics of deflection. Paula
is one of those people, and one of those authors, whose
books are always gently but relentlessly asking us to
prepare for and accept this time for embracing. The
time for doing this work is always now for her, as she
knows better than most that the universe can shift in a

second, and you can be without those you love — so now is the time to embrace pain and learn about love.

But there is some relief in knowing that we can do this at our own pace. In fact, as Paula repeatedly points out in this book, we *have* to perform this art of embracing pain at our own pace. Do it too fast, and it doesn't deepen us into the people we want to become; we look fine externally but we are not fine on the inside. Do it too slow, and we miss what life has to offer. So we must find our own pace. And journey with others who are finding their pace. Hopefully this book will help you do both. It did me.

Roy M. Carlisle
Senior Editor

Of Related Interest

Harold Ivan Smith
GRIEFKEEPING
Learning How Long Grief Lasts

Harold Ivan Smith is a popular speaker and grief educator. He received a doctorate of pastoral care from Rice Seminary and a doctorate of spiritual formation from Asbury Theological Seminary. He is a member of the National Storytellers Association as well as a member of the Association for Death Education and Counseling and the National Hospice Association's Council of Professionals. Smith has written more than thirty books on issues of grief and loss. Comprehensive in scope, *Grief Keeping* is also distinctive for Smith's ability to use true stories and anecdotes from history to illustrate the subject, including ones from the lives of American presidents and their families. Chapters include: The Right to Keep Your Grief; You Have Permission to Grieve as Long as You Need; You Have Permission to Ignore the Stages of Grief; You Have Permission to Lament; Be Angry at God; To Hope; Reinvent Yourself; Support Your Family; Remember Your Dead.

0-8245-2258-3, paperback, 256 pages

crossroad

Also by Paula D'Arcy

THE GIFT OF THE RED BIRD
A Spiritual Encounter

"I was deeply moved by this beautiful true story, and you will be too." — Madeleine L'Engle

"To say that *The Gift of the Red Bird* moved me deeply seems inadequate. I wept for its beauty, pain, and joy. It is a powerful testimony to how the Divine woos the soul into a sacred embrace. Paula D'Arcy's vulnerability and courage in narrating her true story of this Divine encounter are remarkable." — Joyce Rupp

0-8245-1956-6, paperback, 152 pages

Please support your local bookstore,
or call 1-800-707-0670 for Customer Service.

For a free catalog, write us at

THE CROSSROAD PUBLISHING COMPANY
16 Penn Plaza – 481 Eighth Avenue, Suite 1550
New York, NY 10001

Visit our website at
www.crossroadpublishing.com
All prices subject to change.

crossroad